Bloom's
GUIDES

John Steinbeck's
The Grapes of Wrath

1984
The Adventures of Huckleberry Finn
All the Pretty Horses
Beloved
Brave New World
The Chosen
The Crucible
Cry, the Beloved Country
Death of a Salesman
The Grapes of Wrath
Great Expectations
Hamlet
The Handmaid's Tale
The House on Mango Street
I Know Why the Caged Bird Sings
The Iliad
Lord of the Flies
Macbeth
Maggie: A Girl of the Streets
The Member of the Wedding
Pride and Prejudice
Ragtime
Romeo and Juliet
The Scarlet Letter
Snow Falling on Cedars
A Streetcar Named Desire
The Things They Carried
To Kill a Mockingbird

Bloom's
GUIDES

John Steinbeck's
The Grapes of Wrath

Edited & with an Introduction
by Harold Bloom

CHELSEA HOUSE
P U B L I S H E R S
A Haights Cross Communications Company
Philadelphia

A Haights Cross Communications Company ®

www.chelseahouse.com

Contributing editor: Sarah Robbins
Cover design by Takeshi Takahashi
Layout by EJB Publishing Services

Printed and bound in the United States of America.

First Printing
1 3 5 7 9 8 6 4 2

Library of Congress Cataloging-in-Publication Data
John Steinbeck's The grapes of wrath / [compiled by] Harold Bloom.
   p. cm. — (Bloom's guides)
 Includes bibliographical references and index.
 ISBN 0-7910-8239-3 (alk. paper)
 1. Steinbeck, John, 1902-1968. Grapes of wrath. 2. Migrant agricultural laborers in literature. 3. Rural families in literature. 4. California—In literature. 5. Labor camps in literature. 6. Depressions in literature. I. Title: Grapes of wrath. II. Bloom, Harold. III. Series.
 PS3537.T3234G8557 2005
 813'.52—dc22
                2004027519

Contents

Introduction

HAROLD BLOOM

The Grapes of Wrath is a flawed but permanent American book, and its continued popularity, after well more than half a century, seems to indicate that it is anything but a period-piece. In the age of George W. Bush and his allies, the Christian Right, Steinbeck's prose epic has a fresh capacity to offend our pillars of Society. Steinbeck's Okies are detached by him from traditional Protestantism and believe instead in a curious but very American religion of their own, in which the lapsed minister Jim Casy is a secular Jesus Christ and his survivor, Tom Joad, is a kind of St. Paul of social rebellion. Though Steinbeck's prose is perpetually imbued with the King James Bible (and Hemingway), Casy's own Bible reduces to a single book, Ecclesiastes or the Preacher, the most skeptical writing that is canonized as part of the Hebrew Bible or Christian Old Testament. Casy's radical and naturalistic humanism has clear sources in Ralph Waldo Emerson's vision of the Oversoul and in Walt Whitman's love of the democratic masses, yet its darker overtones derive from the tragic Preacher of Ecclesiastes. When Jim Casy declares the holiness of human sexuality or of breakfast, he does not rely upon God as his authority, and Tom Joad does not become an outcast prophet in the name of a Lord who is trampling out the vintage where the grapes of wrath are stored. Tom Joad, American in his self-reliance, will stamp them out for himself, and for those dispossessed with him.

As an American epic, *The Grapes of Wrath* never loses its polemical edge, which is a populist rather than Marxist. The English novelist Anthony Burgess, who recognized shrewdly that Hemingway was Steinbeck's trouble, noted also that Steinbeck was precisely what he asserted himself to be, a Jeffersonian Democrat. I myself tend to think of Steinbeck as the Harry Truman of American novelists: kindly, honorable, pugnacious, and opposed to all forces of exploitation. The shadow of Hemingway hovers over every descriptive passage in *The Grapes of Wrath*, yet for once the book is wholly Steinbeck's own. There is nothing of Hemingway in its stance towards America, though the prose filters the King James Bible's rhetoric through Hemingway's mode of writing about the object-world. As has been noted frequently by critics, the women of *The Grapes of Wrath* are stronger than the men, except for the prophets Jim Casy and Tom Joad, and yet they are not the devouring women of Hemingway and of Scott Fitzgerald. The endurance of Ma Joad and of Rose of Sharon is one of the ornaments of *The Grapes of Wrath*.

Why should the best of Steinbeck's women seem less overdetermined than the men, or quite simply, why does Ma Joad have more freedom of the will than her son Tom does? Why are Steinbeck's men more of a social group, their fates settled by economics, when his outstanding women are able to manifest an acute individuality? Is Ma Joad's passion for keeping her hard-pressed family together merely an instinctual reflex? Certainly, without her will and drive, Tom Joad would not have had the desire to carry on for the martyred Jim Casy. One could argue that *The Grapes of Wrath* weakens as it approaches its conclusion and that only Ma Joad keeps this trailing-off from becoming an aesthetic catastrophe. Confused as Steinbeck becomes, mixing allegorical and ironic elements into a previously realistic plot, the consistency of Ma Joad helps the novelist firm up an otherwise wavering structure. It is curious that rereading the novel can be a less rewarding experience than reseeing the film, where the young Henry Fonda's performance as Tom Joad compensates for some of the contradictions built into the character. The achieved pathos of Fonda's acting helps obscure Steinbeck's inability to persuade us that Tom Joad ends with a more fully articulated sense of identity than he possessed at the onset of the story.

Steinbeck's naturalistic humanism itself seems confused: do his characters fall into animal-like behavior because of society's oppressions, or because they simply revert to their true identity when they are uprooted? Morale is a category that has validity in Hemingway, where you can show courage and assert your dignity against grave odds or else collapse into a failure of nerve. Steinbeck, Hemingway's involuntary disciple, generally cannot keep so clear a vision as to whether the human will is significantly free or not. Ma Joad tells us that the people go on, despite all the injustices that they suffer; we come to believe that the Joads go on mostly because of her firm matriarchal will. Perhaps Steinbeck's true strength in this too-ambitious novel is that the spirit of Ecclesiastes is more movingly incarnated in Ma Joad than in the prophets Jim Casy and Tom Joad. She, and to a lesser extent Rose of Sharon, have the indestructible endurance that rises up from the wisdom of an ultimate skepticism, one that expects nothing and so cannot know defeat.

Biographical Sketch

On February 27, 1902, John Steinbeck was born in Salinas, California, the only son of John Ernst and Olive Steinbeck—a flour-mill manager and schoolteacher. After graduating from high school in June of 1919, while the Great War was drawing to a close, he set out for Stanford University and quickly gained a reputation for being a libertine. During the summers he worked in Salinas as a maintenance man and a ranch hand. He dropped out of school during the middle of his sophomore year and took a bus to San Francisco with Jack London-inspired hopes of boarding a Far East-bound vessel. Soon enough, however, he realized his inexperience and lack of direction and returned to the Salinas Valley. During his time back home, Steinbeck found odd jobs with which to sustain himself; in doing so he picked up material which he would later use in books such as *The Pastures of Heaven* and *The Long Valley*. He reapplied for admission to Stanford for the winter of 1923, and when he was accepted, he fell into a literary-minded crowd and published two stories in the *Stanford Spectator* before deciding that he had endured "all of college I deserve" and needed to run away. In 1925, Steinbeck became preoccupied with getting to New York City—with the publication of Fitzgerald's *The Great Gatsby* and the lure of Greenwich Village adding to his impetus. His means of travel was by way of a friend's house on Lake Tahoe and then a job on a ship headed through the Panama Canal to New York. His uncle Joe helped him get a job at the New York *American*, though in time the lures of city life began to get the better of Steinbeck, his work slackened, and his supervisors fired him. He seized this opportunity to write a series of stories, which were later rejected on the principle that short stories from an unknown writer were not marketable. Desperate for money, he took a job as a steward on a freight ship to San Francisco, and returned to California once again. On another trip to Tahoe he met his future wife Carol Henning, and the nature that surrounded him fueled his interest in Thoreau and naturalism and inspired his first novel, *Cup of Gold*.

In mid-January 1929, a wire came to announce that Robert M. McBridle & Company had accepted *Cup of Gold* for publication. A year later he and Carol were married in a haphazard, spur-of-the-moment ceremony; they rented a shack on the way to Laguna Beach for 15 dollars a month and set up domestic life and writing work among a close-knit circle of friends. That fall, in the waiting room of a dentist's office, Steinbeck met Edward F. Ricketts, who would later serve as an intellectual companion and an inspiration for six novels, including *The Grapes of Wrath*. At Ricketts' urging, Steinbeck examined the dialogue of the fishermen, winos, and businessman who lived and worked along Cannery. The two would sit up into the night and discuss philosophy of the individual versus the collective. *The Pastures of Heaven* was published in November 1932, and Steinbeck's Monterey was expanding to include mythologist and cultural scholar Joseph Campbell, who had an affair with Carol.

1933 brought trouble to the country and to Steinbeck, whose parents' health declined, prompting his return to Salinas. *To a God Unknown* was published in the fall, and Steinbeck retreated into the composition of *Tortilla Flat*, avoiding his wife. He also published two sections of *The Red Pony* in *North American Review*. *Tortilla Flat*'s initial rejection diverted Steinbeck's attention to short stories, one of which, "The Murder," earned the O. Henry prize. Around this time Steinbeck became more and more involved with the situation of the migrant workers in the area and visited with several prominent social reformers, including muckraker Lincoln Stevens and union leader Cicil McKiddy, who became an inspiration for the book *In Dubious Battle* and arguably for Tom's character in *The Grapes of Wrath*.

Meanwhile, in Chicago, publisher Pascal Covici agreed to publish his work, including *Tortilla Flat*, which appeared five days after Steinbeck's father's death. The firm Covici-Friede published *In Dubious Battle* in early 1936, and Steinbeck began work on *Of Mice and Men*. That summer, he agreed to write a series of pieces for the *San Francisco News* about migrant farmers in California, "The Harvest Gypsies." *Of Mice and Men* was published during the winter of 1937; it was adapted into a play by George S. Kaufman, which opened to great reviews the following February. He finished the novella *L'Affaire Lettuceberg*, a precursor to *The Grapes of Wrath*, in late April 1938, burned the manuscript and began anew in May, keeping a diary of his work. Soon after he published *The Long Valley*—a book of stories, the last of which is part of *The Red Pony*—he finished *The Grapes of Wrath*. The exposure surrounding this publication piqued Hollywood interest, and Steinbeck moved to Los Angeles. There he tried to escape marital problems and began an affair with young Gwendolyn Conger. *The Grapes of Wrath* became the best-selling book of 1939 and garnered the Pulitzer Prize shortly thereafter. Steinbeck, Ricketts, Carol, and others embarked on a trip to study the coastal waters off San Francisco and the shoreline of Baja California. The result would be the *Sea of Cortez*, published in 1941. In the meantime, Steinbeck worked for Hollywood and met with President Roosevelt to suggest a propaganda effort to unite the antifascist nations.

Steinbeck left Carol—and California—to set up a life on the East coast and set to work on his next novel, *The Moon is Down*. More wartime projects followed, including *Bombs Away: The Story of a Bomber Team*, and the scripts *A Medal for Benny* and *Lifeboat*. Steinbeck and Gwendolyn—Gywn—were married in March 29, 1943, and soon after, he took the opportunity to work overseas as a war correspondent. Thom Steinbeck was born in New York in August, and *Cannery Row* was published in January 1945, as the Battle of the Bulge was drawing to a close. John Steinbeck IV was born in June of 1946, and the doting father continued to work furiously in his basement, dictating into a tape recorder. *The Wayward Bus* appeared in 1947, and a trip to Russia with photographer Robert Capa resulted in the publication of *A Russian Journal* the following year. While Steinbeck was in Russia, *The Pearl* was released, simultaneously as a book and movie.

After his return from Russia, Steinbeck learned that Ed Ricketts was killed in a car accident. Gwyn asked for a divorce and began what would be a long struggle over children and money. Distraught and unable to focus on his big novel he turned his attention toward an Emiliano Zapata film project, spearheaded by Elia Kazan. He was elected to the Academy of Arts and Letters, and he began seeing Elaine Scott, a former actress and stage manager; she introduced Steinbeck to Rogers and Hammerstein, who bought the rights to a new play Steinbeck was working on, *Burning Bright*. Elaine and John were married on December 28, and Steinbeck returned from his honeymoon dedicated to working on *East of Eden*—a family history for the benefit of Thom and John. While in Spain with his wife Steinbeck heard that Kazin had testified before the House Committee on Un-American Activities, and he defended his friend. After visits to Italy, France, and England, they flew back to New York right before the publication of *East of Eden*. It immediately climbed to the top of the New York Times bestseller list. In 1955, after the release of *Sweet Thursday*, by Rogers and Hammerstein, Steinbeck began working as editor-at-large at *Saturday Review*. His play *Pipe Dream* opened on Broadway, and when he finished *The Short Reign of Pippin IV* he told his editor that he wanted to retell the Knights of the Round Table in English, effectively recasting Malory. He and Elaine lived and worked in Somerset, England, for awhile, and returned reluctantly to New York in 1959.

After so much time abroad, Steinbeck set off on a zig-zag tour of the country in 1960, which resulted in *Travels with Charley*. He and Elaine took his boys on a trip around the world, and were accompanied by a young Irish playwright named Terrence McNally. Steinbeck's ill health cut the trip short, and though they hoped things would calm down, Steinbeck journeyed to Stockholm later that year to accept the Nobel Prize for literature. The Steinbecks continued traveling and were in Warsaw when they learned that Kennedy was shot; later Mrs. Kennedy wrote to Steinbeck asking if he'd write the official biography of her husband. They exchanged letters back and forth, but eventually Steinbeck said that he wouldn't be able to do such a thing. Steinbeck appeared at the White House to receive the Presidential Medal of Freedom in

September of 1964, and Johnson asked him for help on his acceptance speech at the upcoming Democratic convention. This friendship he sustained until the end of his life, though he was torn between logic and his loyalty to the president during the Vietnam War. *Newsday* sent him there as a war correspondent, which led to his "Letters to Alicia." He returned with a serious back injury and confusion about how he might explain his feelings about the war to President Johnson. His health only declined from there, and he passed away quietly, Elaine by his side, on December 20, 1968.

The Story Behind the Story

John Steinbeck's long journey with *The Grapes of Wrath* began during the fall of 1933, when he took long walks around Salinas, to gain relief from the stresses of caring for his dying parents. There he encountered the beat-up cars from Oklahoma, stacked to the hilt with furniture and other possessions and bound west. One day Steinbeck visited a shantytown outside Salinas, which had been dubbed "Little Oklahoma" by the locals, and heard the people's stories. "There's a novel here somewhere," he later told his wife, Carol. (Benson, 286) Though several novels were to come first, Steinbeck's fascination with the plight of the migrant farm workers would continue through the end of the decade and beyond. Indeed, it was difficult for a resident of the California's Central Valley to ignore the influx of people to the area—by the end of the decade, the number of Dust Bowl refugees had been estimated at three or four hundred thousand. (Benson, 335)

During August 1936, not long after the publication of *In Dubious Battle*, Steinbeck was visited by George West, an editor of the *San Francisco News*, who commissioned him to write a series of pieces about the migrant farmers in California. Steinbeck immediately began his task, driving his "pie wagon"—an old bakery truck—in order to look as inconspicuous as possible. He worked with officials of the government's Resettlement Administration, and spent a good deal of time in the San Joaquin Valley with regional director Eric H. Thomsen, who wanted to show him the difference between migrants' quality of life in government camps and on their own. In Maryville Steinbeck encountered Tom Collins, the manager of one of the first Resettlement Administration "demonstration camps," designed to be used as blueprints for growers and local government. Collins inspired Steinbeck so profoundly that *The Grapes of Wrath* was dedicated in part "To Tom, who lived it." Collins, who wore a frayed white suit, like the novel's character Jim Rawley, kept extensive documentation of his experiences in the camps, from the hardships to the entertainment, and such reports informed much of Steinbeck's writing.

Steinbeck finished the seven pieces for the News, each one dealing with a different aspect of the migrant experience and collectively titled "The Harvest Gypsies." After the hubbub surrounding *Of Mice and Men*'s Broadway debut died down, the writer planned a journey west along Route 66, tracing the migrants' path and hooking up with Collins in Gridley, where he was working. By midwinter he was at work on *The Grapes of Wrath*, taking occasional trips back to the camps, including a *Life* magazine commissioned trip to the Visalia region, where a flood brought about starvation and sickness beyond Steinbeck's scope of imagination. The Simon J. Lubin society reprinted Steinbeck's News articles in a pamphlet entitled *Their Blood is Strong*, which drew further attention to the scope of the problem in California.

Steinbeck's interest in the Salinas lettuce strike of 1936 and his anger at the entire situation fueled the completion of *L'Affaire Lettuceberg*, which many consider to be a "dry run" for *The Grapes of Wrath*. Steinbeck himself did not have faith in the novella, which satirized the banks and other anti-labor forces who threatened the migrant workers. His wife Carol, who described it as a "series of cartoons caricaturing Salinas fat cats," (Benson 348), suggested he burn it. Burn it he did, and he began in mid-May, alternating chapters of exposition and narrative, and working furiously. The new title of the book, *The Grapes of Wrath*, was decided upon in September of 1938—it was taken from the *Battle Hymn of the Republic*. He finished the book in late October, consumed by sickness and hoping he'd achieved something "good."

Steinbeck's editor, Pat Covici, wrote that he was "emotionally exhausted upon finishing the work," but the ending he found highly controversial. Debate about this scene, and the decisions Steinbeck made therein, continues today. Critic Nicholas Visser deemed "radical" Steinbeck's choice: the character Rose of Sharon, after having given birth to a stillborn baby, which is sent down the river in an apple box, holds the head of a starving man of her breast, in an attempt to share the milk of human kindness. Despite the disputes over the image of this character as a modern Madonna, Steinbeck insisted that this image had been with him from the novel's outset, and that the strangers the Joads encounter toward the end could not possibly be integrated earlier.

When *The Grapes of Wrath* was first published, it was received more as historical documentation and as popular reading matter than work of true literary merit. Though it has many influences—the Biblical structures and the interchapters reminiscent of works by writers as contemporary to Steinbeck as John Dos Passos—the structure is somewhat unique. Critics such as Kenneth Burke, Edmund Wilson, and Frederic J. Hoffman thought the novel dishonest. It was criticized as well for its lack of organization and its unrealistic dialogue. According to Steinbeck scholar Peter Lisca, these responses were more assertive than analytical. For the topic was likely too close to them, and the presentation too universal, for critics to consider this a work of literature instead of one of social commentary. Indeed, Alfred Kazin called the book "The most influential social novel of the period." But again, this statement of praise does not necessarily mean that he celebrated the fictive qualities of the work; in fact, in the same essay, he deemed its characters unrealistic. Still, the endurance of the book that Lisca called "a great American novel in every sense of the phrase," is undeniable. In the United States alone, 50,000 copies are sold every year.

List of Characters

Tom Joad: The central character of the novel, Tom Joad, a recently released inmate imprisoned for murder, returns home to find that his family has lost their farm and is moving west to California. Tom is a well-meaning man, but he has quick, passionate, and sometimes violent reactions. As his family struggles to survive in worsening circumstances, Tom focuses his energy on helping to organize and help those migrant families in need.

Ma Joad: In some ways the strongest character in the novel, Ma Joad is mother to Noah, Tom, Rose of Sharon, Ruthie, and Winfield. Her love is not demonstrated by acts of affection, but by pragmatism, plain speech, and an unshakable willingness to help those less fortunate. She often places herself in uncomfortable situations for the benefit of the family; as the situation in California worsens, she realizes that the meaning of "family" actually encompasses all of mankind.

Pa Joad: The head of the Joad household, Pa is an Okalahoma sharecropper who has been evicted from his farm. He's a plain-spoken, hardworking man with a spark of mischief, but as the novel progresses, he is frustrated by his inability to control the situation for his family. He is forced to rely on Ma Joad to steer the family and to take a hard line, and this reversal of gender roles frustrates him.

Uncle John: When the Joads first lose their farm, they seek shelter with Pa's brother John, who lost his wife to appendicitis after only four months of marriage; the guilt he felt then has been transferred to a feeling of responsibility for all the family's problems. He is often a morose addition to the caravan West, oscillating between severe self-denial and dangerous indulgence. "He ate little drank nothing, and was celibate," Steinbeck writes. "But underneath his appetites swelled into pressures until they broke through.... when one of his appetites was sated he was sad and ashamed and lonely again." (124)

Rose of Sharon: Tom Joad's younger sister, recently married to Connie Rivers and pregnant with his child, Rose of Sharon begins the journey West with an almost childlike sense of optimism in the future. "The world was pregnant to her," Steinbeck writes. "She thought only in terms of reproduction and motherhood." (123) She dreams constantly of a middle-class life with her husband and her baby, but when her husband leaves her with no warning, she becomes more and more paranoid and disillusioned.

Connie Rivers: The nineteen-year-old husband of Rose of Sharon, he is ambitious and irrational, and regards his young wife with pride, greed, and fear. Connie dreams of taking correspondence courses that will provide him with job opportunities and the possibility of a better life, and he promises Rose of Sharon comfort, cleanliness, and adequate healthcare for their newborn. But when he finds the scenario in California much worse than he expected, he simply disappears from Rose of Sharon's life forever.

Noah Joad: The eldest of the Joad children, Noah is "tall and strange, walking always with a wondering look on his face, calm and puzzled. He had never been angry in his life ... moved slowly, spoke seldom ... people thought he was stupid." (101) This "strangeness" was perhaps the cause of an incident at birth, when Pa, a frightened young father, attempted to extract the baby's head using force. Noah leaves the family at the California border, content to remain an outsider and live off the land—he leaves the burden of explanation to Tom.

Al Joad: Tom's younger brother, Al is a gifted mechanic and dreams of owning his own garage one day. He's equally drawn to young girls. As his family's situation worsens, he is often unable to reconcile necessary sacrifices, such as giving up meat in order that one of his brothers and sisters might benefit from another crucial foodstuff. Since he has the most knowledge of the family's sole means of transportation, he worries that he will be to blame if something goes awry. By the end of the novel he becomes engaged to Aggie Wainwright, and Ma worries that the two will attempt to make their way alone before spring comes to California.

Ruthie Joad: Tom's twelve-year-old sister is tomboyish and forceful, though she "felt the might, the responsibility, and the dignity of her developing breasts." (123) One afternoon fight over a box of Cracker Jack results in Ruthie's admission that Tom is responsible for the murder at Hooper Ranch—this slip forces him to leave the family to avoid the police.

Winfield Joad: The youngest of the Joad clan, ten-year-old Winfield is "kid-wild and calfish ... a trifle of a snot nose, a little of a brooder back of the barn, and an inveterate collecter and smoker of snipes." (123) When the family struggles to feed themselves by picking peaches at the Hooper Ranch, Winfield becomes severely ill from deprivation, though some hard-won milk from the ranch store sets him on the road to recovery.

Grampa Joad: Pa Joad's father, Grampa is "like a frantic child, and the whole structure overlaid with amusement ... he drank too much, ate too much, talked too much." (100) His pride in his family's heritage on the farm results in a protest so forceful that the family must drug him to get him onto the truck. Once the journey commences, he quickly becomes ill, and he dies of a stroke before they even cross the Oklahoma border.

Granma Joad: Her husband's equal in so many ways, Gramna Joad "had survived only because she was as mean as her husband. She held her own with a shrill ferocious religiosity that was as lecherous and as savage as anything Grampa could offer." She often implores Jim Casy, a former preacher, to pray for her family; after her husband's death her health quickly declines—she dies just as the family crosses into California.

Reverend Jim Casy: The former town preacher who has lost his faith as a result of temptation, Jim Casy encounters a just-freed Tom Joad under a willow tree and immediately begins discussing his idea that holiness comes from collective society. His gratitude toward the Joads is so great that when a fight breaks out in the Hooverville, Casy takes the fall for the Joads. Tom later encounters Casy among labor organizers outside a ranch, and later that night, Casy is murdered in a confrontation with police.

Muley Graves: Muley Graves's wife and children leave Oklahoma for California after they lose their home and farmland, but Muley decided to remain in the place he was born, lurking in the carcasses of the farmhouses like a "graveyard ghost" and attempting to elude the police for his constant trespassing. After Tom leaves prison he encounters Muley on his family's property, and Muley tells Tom of his family's misfortune and whereabouts.

Sairy and Ivy Wilson: After the Joads encounter her family in Bethany, Oklahoma, Sairy does her best to comfort them as Grampa sickens and eventually passes away. But Sairy herself is sick, her "face wrinkled as a dry leaf and eyes that seemed to flame in her face, black eyes that seemed to look out of a well of horror. She was small and shuddering." (172) She and Ivy, a middle-aged man from Galena, Texas, accept the Joads' offer to travel as a group to California, and Al helps them when their car breaks down. They continue on until Sairy's ill health forces them to remain at a camp, at the risk of being accused of trespassing.

Floyd Knowles: He befriends Al Joad in the Hooverville when the two young men commiserate over automobiles. His frustration about the lack of work and his family's dire situation leads him to start a fight with a contractor.

Aggie Wainwright: Not long after the Joads begin working in the cotton fields and sharing a boxcar with the Wainwright family, young Aggie falls in love with Al Joad. This initially disturbs Aggie's parents, who are concerned that an illegitimate child could bring shame onto the family, but soon after a conversation between the Joads and the Wainwrights, Al boastfully announces that he and Aggie are engaged to be married.

Summary and Analysis

The Grapes of Wrath starts with the land—the red and gray land, turning cracked and dry—and the young corn, bending slow and despondently back toward the earth. The narrator's eye rises from the ground, as wind kicks dust from the earth and the sharecroppers cower inside their small houses, fearing for the land that is their lifeblood. The time is the 1930s, the place the Oklahoma Dust Bowl. A young man in stiff, cheap clothes approaches a truck and begs a ride from a driver who's just leaving a restaurant. The driver complies and learns the young hitchhiker is bound for his father's 40-acre farm. "And he ain't been dusted out and he ain't been tractored out?" (12) asks the incredulous driver. The young man says he hasn't heard, produces a pint of whisky, and introduces himself as Tom Joad. As they near Joad's destination, the driver's questions provoke the increasingly agitated young man; upon climbing out of the truck, Tom leans back into the window and informs the driver that he was imprisoned for homicide and released early for good behavior. As **chapter 3** opens, a land turtle pushes his way across a steep highway embankment, fighting off red ants and struggling away from a tangle of wild oats. The going gets easier once he reaches the summit, but once he hits the road, a sedan swings off the highway to avoid hitting him. Then a truck takes a deliberate swing at him, sending him upside down and flailing. But slowly his legs emerge; he rights himself on a piece of quartz and continues on his path, staring ahead toward his destination.

These first few chapters of Steinbeck's novel establish the tone, theme, and structure of the work. Desperation seems to swirl and infiltrate the shabby homes in which anxious women stand by their men to await the dust storms. The universality of both Chapter 1 and Chapter 3 establishes Steinbeck's use of the interchapter, a technique that accounts for about one-sixth of the novel and addresses both the setting and circumstance of the novel in a poetic, philosophical tone. These are panoramic, descriptive chapters, in which the narrator functions almost as a

Greek chorus, delivering information about the sharecroppers' reactions to losing their land or the evolution of the land itself. Sometimes the chapters consist of snippets of dialogue and vignettes, through which readers may gain an understanding of that which confronted people like the Joads. Steinbeck scholar Peter Lisca says that this device "is reminiscent of the medieval mystery plays which dramatized Bible stories and made them real to common people." (Con Davis 51) While some critics insist that these interchapters add a sense of chaotic inconsistency to the novel, others, such as Warren French and Mary Ellen Caldwell, think the "chapters have unified and strengthened the whole in theme by the imagery and recurrent motifs deployed in them." (Con Davis 111)

Symbolism is prevalent in this book, and animal imagery is one that will be carried throughout the novel. Critic Brian E. Railsback suggests that a Darwinian approach is evident from the beginning—humans are merely a small part of the picture here, and the land turtle is the most extensive metaphor for the migrant worker, undefeatable, even with a nick on the shell, and bound west at all costs. In this world, Steinbeck seems to suggest, there are those that will go out of their way to make your passage a bit easier, as well as those who will plow into you for no discernable reason. Stuart L. Burns says that the actions and even the physical makeup of the turtle, who is first introduced in Chapter 3, foreshadow the plight of the Joad family. For example, Tom's new yellow, shoes, issued by the prison upon his release, are contrasted with the turtle's toenails.

In **chapter 4**, Tom Joad hears the truck sputter away and slips off his new shoes. He plods along, noting the barbed wire fences and the sagging corn stalks, and scooping up a land turtle he's encountered along the path. As the turtle flails Tom strokes its clean, yellow underside. He continues on, dragging his heels in the dust, until he approaches a dusty willow tree and an emaciated man sitting in its shade. When Tom takes a seat next to the man he asks, "Now ain't you young Tom Joad?" (25) Tom recognizes the man as the preacher Jim Casy, though when he addresses the man as a preacher, Casy insists he "Ain't got the call no more. Got a lot of sinful idears—but they seem kinda sensible." (26) Tom offers his bottle of whisky, and the two share it as Casy explains that his fall from grace began with his desire to bed those women he'd "saved" in prayer meetings. His philosophy evolved further as he realized that " 'Maybe it ain't a sin. Maybe it's just the way folks is ... maybe that's the Holy Sperit—the human sperit—the whole shebang. Maybe all men got one big soul ever'body's a part of.' " (30-31) Tom admits to Casy that he was imprisoned in McAlester for killing a man in self-defense at a dance and invites him back to his family's home. As they near the property, Tom surveys it, reminiscing. In **interchapter 5**, faceless landowners and banks come to evict tenant farmers, who protest that they have nowhere else to go. Tractors come over the roads and into the fields like insects; one man drives a tractor straight through a family's home, on his way to the fields beyond. Casy and Tom survey the Joad place, smashed at one corner and boarded up. They search the grounds and find no one inside; Tom sees a pair of his mother's old shoes, and concludes that the family has left or they've died. He finally unpacks the turtle, which heads "southwest, as it had been from the first." (56) The men stumble upon Muley Graves, who tells Tom his family is at his Uncle John's place, chopping cotton and preparing to set out for the west. Tom suggests that they spend the night at Muley's place, but Muley admits that his wife and children took off for California, and he refused to go. He produces three rabbits from his coat and offers the other two men some, saying "if a fella's got somepin to eat an' another fella's hungry—why, the first fella ain't got no choice." (63) As they eat, Muley confesses that he's haunting the place because all his memories rest there, and Tom tells the story of the murder he's committed and says that he's been paroled and therefore is unable to leave the state. They hear a car in the distance—when Muley says it's the superintendent looking for him, they retreat to sleep in a cave, which Tom once dug with his older brother Noah, as predatory birds circle overhead.

As Casy begins to describe the change he's felt during the past few years, he establishes a philosophy of transcendentalism that will evolve with both Casy, Tom, and the entire Joad family for the duration of the novel. Critic Frederic I. Carpenter suggests parallels between the character of Casy and Ralph Waldo Emerson, who, a century earlier, had given up the ministry because of his own unorthodoxy and who began to associate his religious feelings with nature. Carpenter draws the corollary between Casy's and Emerson's associations of unity with holiness: "As Emerson phrased it, while discussing Nature: "The world lacks unity because man is disunited with himself.... Love is its demand." (Carpenter 317) This philosophy is reflected when Casy discusses his revelations about the "Holy Sperit and the Jesus road." When **interchapter 5** opens, an immediate juxtaposition is established between the love and respect the tenant farmers feel for the land that's sustained them and the disregard of the landowners, who describe the bank as a living, breathing monster that must be fed. Steinbeck's diction emphasizes the force of the tractors and the callousness of their drivers, who, for reasons of survival or politics, have no more regard for the land than the faceless banks: "Behind the harrows, the long seeders—twelve curved iron penes erected in the foundry, orgasms set by gears; raping methodically, raping without passion." (46) The tractor that's plowed into the anonymous family's home in chapter 5 seems to have paid a visit to the Joad farm in **chapter 6**, for as Tom and Casy descend onto the property, they see the house knocked off its foundation. The turtle finally eludes Tom, "waving his legs and boosing its heavy, high-domed shell along toward the southwest," (57) foreshadowing the Joads' own journey. News from Muley Graves emphasizes the direness of the situation, though he affiliates himself with the "good" woman who swerved to avoid the turtle by sharing his jackrabbit with Casy and Tom.

Interchapter 7 opens upon a used car lot, where salesmen circle, much like the predatory birds with an eye on Muley's cave. The poor tenant farmers bargain and barter for vehicles to take them on to Calfornia. **Chapter 8** begins at dawn, as Casy and Tom hasten their way across the road toward Uncle John's house. Tom discloses that his uncle drinks too much and lives alone after his young wife of four months died of a burst appendix. Tom recognizes his dog Flash and calls him, and as they approach, he sees his father working on a Hudson Super-Six sedan. Tom creeps out slowly, and his father slowly recognizes him. He nervously touches him on the shoulder and invites him inside, yelling to his wife that some men from the road have come for breakfast. Tom watches his mother from afar and reflects on her influence. When she sees him, she's concerned he's escaped; when she's reassured, she rushes to him and gently touches his cheek. As the family is summoned for breakfast, Tom can hear their reactions to the news of his return. Ma Joad explains that her new, fearful attitude has come from the violence of the family's recent displacement. Granma, Grampa, Pa, and Noah approach, and Grampa expresses his pride that they couldn't keep a Joad in jail. Tom introduces Casy and demands that Casy say grace for the benefit of his grandmother. After some confused ramblings about the point and presence of God and holiness, Casy says "I'm glad of the holiness of this breakfast. I'm glad there's love here. That's all." (105) Casy's philosophy is revealed in (Christ's temptation in the wilderness/Transcendentalist philosophy).The family explains that with the money they saved from picking cotton, Tom's younger brother Al bought a Hudson truck for the trip west; his sister Rose of Sharon is married to Connie Rivers and pregnant.

As across Oklahoma farmers become migrants, entire lives are sorted—jewelry, furniture, picture frames, and toys. "Can you live without the willow tree?" implores the narrator. "Well, no, you can't. The willow tree is you. The pain on that mattress there—that dreadful pain—that's you." (115) The Joads pack up the Hudson as they speculate about their future in California—Pa Joad found a handbill advertising work opportunities, which leads the family to believe their fortune will be favorable. Grampa comes out in his pajamas, fumbling with his fly and acting crude. Jim Casy emerges from the barn and asks if he might go west with the Joads—Ma tells him that if the men deem there's room, he's certainly welcome. Bouncing in on the truck comes the rest of the Joad clan: Uncle John, younger brother Al, younger sister Rose of Sharon (pregnant and clutching the hand of her husband, Connie Rivers), and the youngest, Winfield and Ruthie. They climb off the truck frustrated, having only received 18 dollars for the contents of the farm. Later that evening, after Tom has greeted the rest of his family and sufficiently teased his younger siblings, the Joads meet near the truck to take stock of their finances and to determine when they should leave. Al, the most mechanically savvy, gives his advice on the tires. They slaughter a pig and then determine that leaving as soon as possible would be in their best interests. So, carrying slabs of meat into the kitchen for salting and packing up the truck by lantern-light, the family scarcely notices Ma Joad in the kitchen, mournfully deciding which keepsakes to burn and which to put into her pocket. Muley Graves stops by, and Pa offers him a spot in the truck; when he refuses, Grampa insists that he'll stay as well. The family is forced to drug him in order to load him onto the truck and drive away. All across Okalahoma, families leave creaky, vacant homes, confused hunting cats, and bereft land.

The contradictory feelings of Tom's homecoming and the family's inevitable departure set up a struggle in which the Joad family is introduced in the kind of nervous motion that will be sustained throughout the novel. Ma, a woman "thick with childbearing and work," who is immediately introduced as "the citadel of the family," (95) denies emotion by virtue of necessity. Still, when Tom bites his lip until it bleeds, Ma shows a bit of emotion; she deplores Tom not to act out in the ways that he has. The family is introduced quickly, and their characters are developed as they set to work packing the truck and salting the pork. When Ma protests that Casy shouldn't help in the salting process, as its women's work, the preacher replies that "It's all work. They's too much of it to split it up to men's or women's work. You got stuff to do. Leave me salt the meat." (138) Ma's struggle to part with the family's possessions and Grampa's unwillingness to leave the barn must only be temporary distractions—when the load is tethered to the top of the truck, and the family climbs on top, they do not look back.

Highway 66 becomes a temporary home for all these migrants, "from the Mississippi to Bakersfield." (150)

Overloaded trucks strain, and children whine for water. The Joads turn west in the creaking Hudson, as the sun overhead creates mirages. As the family awakens to sunburns, they pass around leftover pork bones upon which to gnaw. They stop to buy gas from an attendant who suspects they have no money and guesses immediately that they're headed to California. Tom takes a turn at the wheel, and the family feasts their eyes on big-city life as they drive through Oklahoma City. When they stop at another service station shack they encounter Ivy and Sairy Wilson, whose car has broken down. Ivy discloses that his wife isn't well, and Grampa says that he's sick too. Sairy, wondering aloud if the man might be having a stroke, invites Grampa into their tent. Granma orders Casy to pray, but Grampa takes a few dying breaths and then lays still. Pa Joad insists that their family is beholden to the Wilsons. Sairy offers to add potatoes to the Joads' pork sand insists that "People needs—to help." (180) Rose of Sharon is concerned that proximity to death will hurt the baby, but Ma insists that a child born out of sorrow is a happy child. They ready the body for burial and demand a prayer of Casy, who utters something short and informal. Ivy Wilson says that he's seen handbills similar to those the Joads are holding and also says that he can't get his car to start. Al offers his mechanical expertise. The families agree to set off together, helping one another, as Ma says, "Each'll help each, an' we'll all git to California." (190)

When the Joads stop for gas, their dog is run over, and Rose of Sharon is distraught, worrying that witnessing such tragedy will have an effect on her baby. When they encounter the Wilsons that night, the theme of hospitality, which was first established when the truck driver agreed to take Tom home, becomes more realized. Critic Barbara Heavilin connects Casy's ideas of a common humanity to the sharing of the migrants family: "The Joads treat others whom they encounter throughout the novel with kindness and hospitality, and other characters well serve to delineate this theme, creating a thread of hospitable action and kindness to strangers." (Heavilin 85) Indeed, Sairy Wilson shares her quilt and her sympathies with

Grampa, while she suffers herself from a sickness that keeps her awake at night.

The Western land and the Western States are nervous under the change, says the narrator, and the result of commiseration such as the Joads' and Wilsons' results in revolution—for the causes, the tractors, are not in themselves bad, but the compounding effects of the landowners and banks are something entirely more dangerous, "for the quality of owning freezes you forever into 'I,' and cuts you off forever from 'we.'" (194) In **interchapter 15**, Cadillacs and Zephyrs sail by the loaded up trucks, and at a hamburger stand, an overloaded 1926 Nash sedan pulls in. A bedraggled man asks the waitress for some water, and she leads them to the hose out back. When he asks if she'll sell them bread, she refuses, until the cook insists she sell it to them. After she haggles with them over price, she gives them an entire loaf for ten cents and then cuts them a deal on candy for the children. Enroute Rose of Sharon confesses to Ma that once they get to California, she and Connie don't want to live in the country with the rest of them. Connie wants to get a house in town, take a correspondence course, and own a store in which she proposes Al might work. When the Wilsons' car breaks down, Al gets frustrated, and the Wilsons propose the Joads travel on without them. Some propose that the group break in two, some to continue and some to repair the Wilsons' car. Ma grabs a jack-handle and demands the family stay together. Since Gramma's health is failing, Al, Tom, and Casy stay to repair the truck while the rest go on in search of a place to camp. Casy tells Tom in conversation that he hopes he'll be able to help all of these people involved in this great migration.

Chapter 15 is the structural center of The Grapes of Wrath, and critic Mary Ellen Caldwell suggests that it is the epitome of the entire book. This interchapter begins with a panoramic view that's similar to that of many other interchapters, but instead of focusing on the land, Steinbeck describes the hamburger stands and gas stations that dot Highway 66. He moves from general description—"Minnie or Susy or Mae, middle-aging behind the counter, hair curled and rouge and powder on a sweating face... The cook is Joe or Carl or Al, hot in a white coat and apron, beady sweat on white forehead, below the white cook's cap ..."—to a specific scene. The waitress, Mae, prefers the truck drivers to the richer folks, the "shitheels," who order only a five-cent soda and complain that it's not cold enough. When a 1926 Nash rattles in, piled to the top, and a man comes in to buy a loaf of bread. Though she first refuses—the stand needs the loaf, which costs more than the family is able to part with—prompted by Al's growling, she agrees, and then sells the children two five-cent candies for a penny. The truck drivers, who have witnessed this exchange, leave a generous tip. "[The Nash] is symbolic of all the jalopies in poor condition being nursed to get to California," writes Caldwell. (Con Davis113) "Al and Mae's stand could have been on any highway. The rich, traveling in highpowered cars, crashed into poor families. The dispossessed and land hungry ones ... wanted work, not charity. Both generosity and selfish conniving came from unexpected sources." (114) Like the Nash, the Wilsons' and Joads' cars "crawl along like bugs." When the idea of splitting up arises, Ma threatens the family with a jackhandle, essentially establishing herself as the head of the family. "Like a bunch of cows, when the lobos are ranging, stick all together," Ma says. "I ain't scared when we're all here, all that's alive, but I ain't gonna see us bust up." (219)

When the Joads finally pull their fixed car into the camp, the proprietor insists they pay to park it. They strike a bargain with the proprietor, and a man on his way back from California tries to tell the Joads what they have in store for themselves. "Took two kids dead, took my wife dead to show me," (245) he insists, shaken. As they leave the shaken man behind, Casy insists that the man probably is telling his own truth, but that such a thing might not mean much for the Joads. They all go off to sleep, some in the car, some in the open. In **interchapter 17** the cars crawl ahead, and every night the migrants set up camp together, unwrapping guitars and sharing means. Laws and punishments are created in these transitional worlds, and they're taken down as easily as tents are in the morning. The Joads move through New Mexico, and a border guard stops them on the way in to Arizona. They continue to crawl through the desert and then stop one hot morning by a river, as they exclaim that they're in California. Tom insists that they still have to get across the desert, but they stop at an encampment near the river to wash. The men swim and run into two more men who speak of the starvation that is ahead for the Joads—they say that there is beautiful land, but it can't be owned; that there are countless oranges, but they can't be eaten. Uncle John tells Pa that since they're on their way, they must continue. As Tom and Noah find a place to sleep for the night, Noah confides in his younger brother that he won't continue with the family. He backs away down the riverbank, insisting that Tom inform Ma. Meanwhile, Ma sits patiently beside Gramma, who's delirious. Ma rejects a Jehovite woman's offer to hold a prayer meeting in their tent, so the woman holds a meeting in another tent. Suddenly Gramma begins to sleep easier, and Rose of Sharon wonders where Connie has gone. A marshal comes into the tent and insists that the family cannot stay where they are, calling them Okies—Ma insists they'll leave in the morning and threatens the man with a skillet.

The next morning Ma discusses the phrase with Tom. Tom uses that moment to break the news that Noah has gone away, down the river, and Ma, distraught over the dissolution of her family, prays they all can get some rest. When Pa hears the news of Noah's disappearance he says "that boy's all my fault." (279) As the Joads prepare to leave before getting in trouble with the police, Ivy Wilson says that Sairy is too sick to continue. When Pa suggests they all stay, Ivy insists they continue. Sairy summons Jim Casy to say a prayer; when he bows his head and then straightens it, she thanks him for the feeling of closeness. The Joads prepare to leave, leaving a skillet of meat and potatoes and two dollars for the Wilsons before they continue toward Needles. They stop at a gas station where they are treated inhumanely by the service station employees, and then continue on, Ma tending to Gramma, and Rose of Sharon and Connie furtively making love. When they stop for inspection, Ma speaks quickly to the guards, insisting that Gramma is sick and needs a doctor. When Tom pulls the car away and inquires about Gramma's condition, Ma insists she's all right and they should keep going. Dawn breaks and they see the orchards, the lush trees—they've made it across. They beg Ma to come out, and when she does, she tells them Gramma's dead.

As the journey west continues, the Joads meet more loss and hardship. Critic Edwin T. Bowden suggests that the isolation of the Okies prompts them to turn within for comfort and strength. When the family circle begins to break, as is the case with the Joad family, it is the nearest thing to actual defeat. Bowden writes: "Some of these losses are inevitable and unavoidable, others are the result of too great an individual weakness, but each tends to lessen the fierce family loyalty and will that carry the Joads through their trials and loneliness." (Con Davis 18) Now that the Joads are in California, with fewer numbers than with which they began, they must face the reality that their images of Eden may not in fact be so realistic. **Interchapter 19** charts the evolution of California, from the hands of the Mexicans to the American "squatters," on to industrial owners who imported slaves and finally storekeepers who "farmed on paper" (299), lost their connection to the land, and exploited workers. One homeless, hungry man drives his wife and starving children to a Hooverville—where raids and sickness and struggle and hope were all typical. Law officers stood guard to destroy any meager crops the migrants might be able to yield from secret, "stolen" patches of land. In **chapter 20**, the Joads emerge from the coroner's office in Bakersfield, where Gramma had a pauper's funeral. They continue on until they reach a Hooverville, where the people seem strange and the system seems chaotic. They set up camp, and as Ma prepares stew, she is stunned by the flock of hungry children who gather around her. Al continues to work on the car as Tom and Casy chat philosophically. Connie tells Rose of Sharon that if he knew the trip would be so bad he never would have come, and that he needs to get back on his feet. As Ma cooks, one small girl tells her about Weedpatch, a government camp with hot water and real toilets and Saturday-night dances. Al meets a young man named Floyd Knowles who's fixing his car. Floyd tells Al and Tom about work two hundred miles north. A shiny sedan sails through the camp, and some well-dressed contractors offer the men work. When Floyd prods them for specifics, a deputy sheriff suggests he's seen Floyd loitering near a used car lot that was robbed. Floyd hits the deputy and Tom trips him, and when the deputy takes a shot at Floyd, he mistakenly shoots the knuckles from a woman's hands. To stop the deputy from shooting again, Casy kicks the man in the neck. When the police come, Casy insists Al and Tom (who will certainly be punished for breaking parole) flee; he takes the blame for the incident and is hauled off to jail. As the guards lead him away, Casy keeps his head held high. "On his lips there was a faint smile and on his face a curious look of conquest." (343)

Feeling depressed about the fate of Casy and the course of his own life, which he believes causes the family's suffering, Uncle John leaves to get drunk. Rose of Sharon realizes that Connie has disappeared, and Tom insists to Ma that the family must leave the camp tonight, as it is to be burned because of the incident. Tom goes to drag a drunk Uncle John home, and Rose of Sharon grows hysterical with disbelief that Connie has actually left her. Ma rebukes Tom for hitting the cop, and as a frustrated Tom turns the family toward a government camp, Ma reminds him that "we're the people that live. They ain't gonna wipe us out." (360) **Interchapter 21** addresses the changes that have been felt by the former sharecroppers, and the frustration that united them. In contrast, those who owned land in the West were wary of these migrants, worried about disease and losing their work and land. "The great companies did now know that the line between hunger and anger is a thin line," the narrator says. "On the highways the people moved like ants and searched for work, for food. And the anger began to ferment." (365) This imagery points to the title of the novel, as like wine made from grapes, the migrants' anger is beginning to turn into something much more potent. Critic Peter Lisca suggests that the wine imagery, present in the novel's title as well as in passages such as these "alludes to

Deuteronomy, Jeremiah, and Revelation, as for example, 'And the angel thrust in his sickle into the earth, and gathered the vine of the earth, and cast it into the great winepress of the wrath of God.'"

The Joads practically run straight into Weedpatch, and a watchman assigns them to Number Four Sanitary Unit, with toilets, showers, and washtubs. They are introduced to the rules of the camp, told that the police are elected and that it's possible to work in exchange for housing. Tom encounters the Wallace family—the young wife prepares breakfast while nursing a baby under her shirtwaist, and Tom accepts their offer to share food. Timothy and Wilkie Wallace take Tom to work with them, and the boss, Mr. Thomas, informs them of a fight to be staged in the camp during the Saturday night dance. Ruthie and Winfield discover the foreign, indoor plumbing, which frightens them; Rose of Sharon whines for Connie, and Ma rustles her to clean herself up, as the Ladies Committee is scheduled to pay the Joads a visit. The camp manager, Jim Rawley, drops in on the Joads first, and asks Ma if he might have a cup of her coffee. This compliment means a lot to Ma, and she feels reassured by both his friendliness and the frayed seams on his clothes. Al comes in with news of a house trailer, which can be driven and lived in; Ma proudly informs Pa of her visitor. Rose of Sharon comes back clean and well-dressed, excited by the notion that in this camp, her baby might be born with the proper care and consideration. As Rose of Sharon stands outside and caresses her stomach, a woman passes and warns her against clutch-and-hug dancing. She says such close contact will cause Rose of Sharon to lose the baby. Her fears are assuaged first by the manager and then by Ma.

The Ladies Committee arrives and introduces themselves with much pomp. They inform Ma of the rules and facilities of the camp, and tell her of a case in which one family was stealing toilet paper. A woman emerges and explains that she has five girls who were eating only green grapes on account of their not having any other food, and their diarrhea was the cause of the toilet paper consumption. Jessie insists the woman go to the Weedpatch store to buy proper groceries with the camp credit, assuring her that she'll pay it back when she gets work. Meanwhile, Ruthie butts her way into a croquet game, causing the rest of the children to flee. When Winfield joins the rest of the children, Ruthie runs home in tears. Pa, Al, and Uncle John look for work, and Uncle John bemoans his aches and pains, saying that he'd like to go away before he brings more punishment on the family. Pa insists that he can't leave, that they've already lost enough of the family. The same woman who warned Rose of Sharon against Saturday night dances, Lisbeth Sandry, approaches the Joads' unit again; she asks if Ma has been saved and again warns against the dances. When Ma insists she leave, Lisbeth continues to fight until Ma picks up a stick and threatens her. At this moment Lisbeth begins howling, drooling, and sinking to her knees; the manager and others come running, informing Ma that the woman's not well. Ma tells the manager that if the woman returns she'll hit her, and the manager begs Ma to try and restrain herself. Pa returns and informs Ma that he hasn't found any work, and together they re-live the sadness they've been too busy to experience.

Steinbeck's portrayal of the Weedpatch camp is modeled after a similar one the author visited while conducting research for the *San Francisco News*. The cleanliness and orderliness of this government camp is a sharp contrast to the Hooverville and provides an example of how people are able to govern themselves when in a hospitable and well-equipped situation. Tom encounters the Wallace family, who are able to share both their food and their work. Barbara Heavilin writes: "Highly memorable and symbolic, this scene brings together the novel's theme of hospitality and of the nurturing mother, a scene to be repeated in the novel's ending, with a twist both sacred and grotesque." (46) Ma immediately notices the change in conditions and in her own perceptions. "These folks is our folks—is our folks," she says incredulously. "An' that manager, he come an' set an' drank coffee ... an' he says, 'Mrs. Joad' this, an' 'Mrs. Joad' that ... Why, I feel like people again." (395) In effect, Ma comments on the healing that is now taking place since the confrontation with the border patrolman in Needles, from whom she first heard the word "Okie." The improved conditions allow for a bit of leisure time, and **interchapter 23** portrays the storytelling that goes on in the camps. One man recounts that he was a recruit for Geronimo and never got over shooting a young Indian brave. Another man described a movie he saw, about two rich people who pretended they were poor so they could find someone to love them. Then the narrator discusses the benefits of drunkenness, the idea that taking the hard edges away from life renders everything holy, even the drinker. Another source of pleasure is the harmonica—easy to carry and versatile in sound—the guitar, and the fiddle. Playing these instruments evokes dancing. The people also take solace in religion and riverside baptism; for the children, the notion of avoiding sin evokes the curious possibility of committing sin.

On Saturday morning, the women of Weedpatch hang out the gingham dresses in preparation for the dance, and in the tent of Ezra Huston, chairman of the central committee, five men meet to discuss the plot to disturb the dance. They plan to keep their eyes and ears open and to thwart any outside plan to start a riot. Slowly cars of invited guests begin to arrive, each driver announcing the name of the camper who invited him. Ruthie and Winfield quickly eat dinner as Ma inspects them for dirt, and Al preens. Tom remarks upon Rose of Sharon's condition, and Ma replies that pregnant women always get prettier. Rose of Sharon frets about the dance and tells Ma that she misses Connie. Ma comforts her and insists she doesn't shame the family—she'll accompany Rose of Sharon to the dance. The dance commences, and the "Entertainment Committee" keeps an eye out for infiltrators. When a scuffle breaks out on the dance floor, Tom and the others remove three men paid to disrupt the dance. Ezra Huston addresses them, realizes they're part of the camp, and asks that they are let go, "They don't know what they're doin'." The squad moves back toward the dance floor, the dance resumes, and Pa and some others muse that a change is a coming, and that they might try to unite against accusers. **Interchapter 25** begins with visions of California's lush, fruitful springtime, but slowly shifts to the reality of waste—overabundance of fruit, overripe fruit, and the starving people who are not allowed to benefit.

The passage concludes: "In the souls of the people the grapes of wrath are filling and growing heavy, growing heavy for the vintage." (449) This interchapter contains perhaps Steinbeck's most well-known lament, for children who die of starvation while oranges rot around them.

The pallor of all the Joads—especially Winfield and Rose of Sharon—has Ma worried and asking the men about their work prospects. Tom suggests that there could be some more work north of the camp, and Ma insists the family pack up their things and move on, despite the relatively luxurious conditions of the camp. When Pa protests about the timing, Ma takes a hard line and rebukes him, in part to keep everyone's spirits up. Rose of Sharon is depressed because she hasn't had milk, as doctors have advised—to keep her spirits up, Ma presents her with the small, gold earrings, piercing her ears as a right of passage. Al says goodbye to a blonde girl, promising her that he'll be back in a month with enough money to take her to the movies. Tom reminisces with Wilkie and Jule, discussing their past experiences and what's in store for the Joads; Ruthie wonders aloud whether there'll be croquet where they're going. At dawn Ma rouses the entire family, presenting them each with a biscuit, as there's nothing else to eat. As they drive past the rebuilt Hooverville and beyond, Ma tells Tom that they'll need a house before the winter rains, as Winfield's health is worsening. They all have individual daydreams of good fortune—of enough food, of hot coffee and tobacco and enough money to see the movies every night. They run into traffic, and note a line of white motorcycles blocking the road. A state policeman asks them if they'd like to work and puts them in a line of cars waiting for the ranch. They are assigned a small, dirty dwelling, and ignoring Rose of Sharon's complaints, they begin to unload. The men are given the rules of the orchards, and Tom's first box of peaches is turned down because of bruising. Winfield and Ruthie also work, as does Ma, who comes late because Rose of Sharon has fainted.

Ma takes the earnings to the ranch store, and discovers prices are much higher than she imagined. She is insistent that Tom has his sugar, and after some debate the clerk takes a dime from his pocket and says Ma can pay him back with the next day's wages. This random act of kindness continues Ma's education into the workings of this new world. "Learnin' it all a time, ever' day," she says to herself, as the screen door swings shut, "If you're in trouble or hurt or in need—go to poor people. They're the only ones that'll help—the only ones." (483) The family returns from work, washes up, and eats—they enjoy the food but wish aloud there was more to be had. Tom goes off by himself and takes a walk to investigate the commotion from that morning. He runs into a man who suggests Tom turn around, lest "them goddamn reds" get him (488). He pretends to go back to his assigned house, then turns around and sneaks under the fence. There he runs into a group of people, among them Jim Casy. They catch up quickly, and Casy urges Tom to send word that once the strike is broken, their wages will go down considerably—from five cents to two and a half cents a box. They sit and talk awhile longer, until suddenly they realize they've been surrounded by the deputies. Casy tries to explain to the deputies that they're killing starving children—but such an utterance provokes a deputy to strike at his head swiftly, killing him instantly. Tom, full of rage, wrenches the club away from the deputy and kills him. Then a club meets his head and Tom begins running. He feels trickles of blood and realizes that his nose is broken. As he hides, he watches dancing beams flash along the highway, and creeps slowly toward the family's house. He puts aside the questions of his mother and his brother and lay in the darkness, his face throbbing, listening to the footsteps of the watchmen. Critic J. Paul Hunter counts Casy's last days as proof that the preacher's ideas bridge the gap from, the Old to the New Testament. He writes: "He embarks upon his mission after a long period of meditation in the wilderness; he corrects the old ideas of religion and justice, he selflessly sacrifices himself for his cause, and when he dies, he tells his persecutors, '"You don' know what you're a doin."'"

When dawn finally comes, Ma dresses, dispatches Pa to get supplies for breakfast, and surveys Tom. When she sees Tom's bloody face, she asks him what has happened. He insists on telling everyone at once, including the children, so that they don't "blab." The story comes out, and, horrified, Ma insists the children answer any questions by saying that Tom is sick, and insists they leave in the morning. Rose of Sharon is hysterical at the thought of Tom killing someone, thinking that such a deed will ruin her chances of having a nice baby. They hear from outside that the pay has indeed dropped to two and a half cents, and Ruthie runs in, reporting that Winfield has collapsed in a field. Ma dispatches a grumbling Pa to fetch milk, and when Al learns that dinner will be cornmeal mush, he is upset as well. Rose of Sharon protests that she needs the milk, and Ma rationalizes that Rose of Sharon is still on her feet. When Winfield finally sits up to eat and drink, Ma sneaks the rest of the milk to Rose of Sharon. Ruthie insists that she'll never admit what Tom has done to anyone. The next morning at dawn they are packing up the truck—Tom hidden under a mattress—when a guard stops them to ask where they're going and what happened to the other man with them. Al lies on behalf of his brother, and they set off. Seeing signs advertising for cotton pickers, they decide that they'll look for work and live in a boxcar while Tom hides in the brush, waiting for his face to heal.

Chapter 27 begins with a hopeful picture of the cotton-picking work—the bags can be positioned so both hands are free to work, and a full bag can be bought for a dollar. There remains distrust, however, between the migrants and the owners; sometimes the migrants load their bags with rocks, and sometimes the owners' scales are fixed. Despite the initial bounty, dark clouds begin to form on the horizon—cotton ruins the land, and winter quickly approaches. The Joads set up camp at one end of a boxcar; every day they picked cotton, and every night they had meat—they even have enough to buy new overalls for the men and a new dress for Ma. Ma is greeted by Mrs. Wainwright, who lives on the other side of the car. Winfield bursts in and tells Ma that Ruthie got into a fight and threatened the other girl by telling her what Tom had done. Heartbroken, Ma asks Rose of Sharon to watch the supper while she goes to tell Tom what's happened. Tom has fashioned a cave between blackberry bushes, and he invites Ma in. He eats the food while Ma tells him that he must leave, since Ruthie's told the children and the children will certainly spread the word. Ma reaches to feel the scar on his face and his crooked nose, and insists that he take seven dollars she's put aside for him. Tom confesses that while he's been hiding he's been thinking about Casy's notion that in hiding out he discovered he was simply one piece of a big soul—he tells Ma that he wants to continue Casy's work. When Ma expresses concern for his safety and asks Tom how she'll know about him, he assures her "I'll be ever'where ... wherever they's a fight so hungry people can eat ... wherever they's a cop beatin' up a guy ..." Critic Mimi Reisel Gladstein says Ma's strength is particularly exemplified in this scene: "She gives him some money that she has been 'squirrelin'' away. When he demurs, her response is a good illustration of how effectively Ma can manipulate people. She tells Tom that he has no right to cause her pain ... her eyes are wet and burning, 'but she did not cry.' Instead she returns to the boxcar to face still more adversity."

Tom's speech to Ma reflects that he has finally picked up the yoke that Casy has left for him, suggesting that for Tom, this new world of struggle requires attention to community more than attention to family. Though in the case of people such as Lisbeth Sandry, who frightens Rose of Sharon with their descriptions of "clutch and hug dancing," religion can be viewed in this novel as a frightening , negative force, it also leads to the practical realization of responsibility to community. When Tom says "I'll be ever'where—wherever you look," he draws upon the words of Jesus, in Matthew: "Behold, I am always with you." After Ma quickly takes leave of her son, she encounters a man who offers her family work at a good price. She insists they'll be there in the morning, and when she returns to the boxcar, she sees Mr. Wainwright and offers them the work as well. Mr. Wainwright expresses his concern that Aggie has been out walking with Al every night; he requests that Al doesn't bring any shame on their family, implying that he doesn't want Aggie to get pregnant, and Ma says that she'll talk to Al. Later she apologizes to Pa for taking such initiative, but Pa is so homesick and nostalgic that he no longer minds. Al comes in and announces that he and Aggie Wainwright are going to marry and go away. Everyone is glad, but Ma begs Al to stay until spring. Rose of Sharon is so upset about Connie that she crawls into the bushes to avoid the festivities.

The family awakens the next morning at dawn, and Rose of Sharon insists on going with them to pick cotton, much to Ma's dismay. When they arrive, they realize that several other families have also heard about the work; the cotton picking is finished by noon, as rain clouds gather in the distance. They climb back in the truck, and Ma realizes that Rose of Sharon has caught a chill. When they return Ma puts the girl's feet in hot water and sends the entire family out to gather wood for a fire. As the family huddles together in the boxcar, the last interchapter begins with gray clouds marching in over the craggy coastal mountains. When the rain began, the migrants wondered how long it would go on. But slowly the rain ruined the cars, mud engulfing the wheels; then the people began to wade away, searching for shelter in high barns, in relief offices, as sickness wracks their families and renders them slowly hopeless. On the second day of the rain Al lays the tarpaulin separating the two families over the nose of the truck, so that the two families become one. On the third day the Wainwrights consider leaving, but Ma reminds them that they have shelter and convinces them to stay. Rose of Sharon, shivering with fever, refuses a cup of hot milk, and Pa and Uncle John consider shoring up the creek so that it won't flood the boxcars. Ma answers the whining of Ruthie and Winfield with promises that they'll soon have a house, a dog, and a cat. Rose of Sharon suddenly cries, and Ma realizes that she's gone into labor early. She shoos the children away with Aggie, but they hide and watch. Pa comes back, and when he realizes the situation, he continues shoveling mud with the men as the steam rises. As evening fell Rose of Sharon screams with the ferocity of the pains and Uncle John threatens to run away.

Finally the screams cease, and a few moments later the bank crashes. Uncle John collapses, the water up to his chest, and Al begins running to try and start the car. Uncle John dismisses Pa as Pa climbs into the car. He is immediately hit with the smell of burning afterbirth and the sight of a shriveled blue baby in an apple box. Uncle John begins sobbing. Pa wonders aloud if they could have done anything more, and Ma insists they did everything. Mrs. Wainwright offers to help so Ma can sleep, and Ma accepts her offer, saying, "Use'ta be the fambly was fust. It ain't so now. It's anybody. Worse off we get, the more we got to do." (569) She lays down next to Rose of Sharon and falls into a fitful sleep, calling for Tom. Mrs. Wainwright asks the men to bury the baby, and Uncle John tries to, but when the water is too deep he lets it float with the current. Pa and Al build a platform from the slats of wood that were on the side of the truck; when Pa fetches groceries, Ma rebukes him for having spent all the money on bread. In the boxcar the family huddles on top of piles as six inches of water seep into the cabin. On the morning of the second day Pa goes off and comes back with ten potatoes to eat. The next morning Ma says the group is going off to higher ground. Al protests, saying he's to stay with Aggie. As they wander down the highway, Ruthie and Winfield argue over a red geranium, and the entire family seeks shelter in a rain-blackened barn. As a huge storm descends on the family, they stagger into the barn. Winfield notices a starving boy and man struggling in the corner. The boy brings a comforter out for Rose of Sharon and explains that his father is starving and asks if they have any milk. Ma's eyes meet her daughter's, and without a question Rose of Sharon agrees, gasping. Ma shoos away the children and the men, and Rose of Sharon lies down next to the starving man, bares her breast, and holds his head to it. She smiles mysteriously, and the novel comes to a close.

The Biblical references in these last few chapters, leading up to the simultaneous climax and ending, are unmistakable—Chapters 29 and 30 are in many ways a prelude to disaster, and they echo in incremental repetition the way things fall apart for the Joads. "On the second day of the rain," the narrator explains, "Al took the tarpaulin down from the middle of the car." (557) This action, and the echo of Genesis in the explanation, unites the Wainwrights and the Joads as one family caught in the same plight. According to critic Warren French, Ma's unspoken suggestion that Rose of Sharon offer her breast to this stranger carries into practice the idea that the worse off people are, the more they have to do. "The tableau in the barn does not halt an unfinished story; it marks the end of the story that Steinbeck had to tell about the Joads. Their education is complete; they have transcended familial prejudices. What happens to them now depends on the ability of the rest of society to learn the lesson that the Joads have learned."(Con Davis, 31). J. Paul Hunter suggests that this final, striking scene not only combines three major symbols of a purified order—the Old Testament deluge, the New Testament stable, and the ritual of Communion—but it combines horror with hope. "Its imitation of the Madonna and child is a grotesque one," Hunter writes, "for it reflects a grotesque world without painless answers, a world where men are hit by axe handles and children suffer from skitters. Steinbeck does not promise Paradise for the Joads." (Con Davis 47) This theme of "the education of the Joads," that has been discussed by critics such as Peter Lisca, is also reflected in this last scene, as Rose of Sharon, arguably one of the most selfish characters from the outset, transforms this energy to a love of family and then, at the end, transcends even that love. "The tragedy of The Grapes of Wrath consists in the breakup of the family," Carpenter writes. "But the new moral of the novel is that the love of all people—if it be unselfish—may even supersede the love of family." (Carpenter 321) This is a sentiment perhaps first uttered aloud by Ma, after she heard the news that Tom had killed someone outside the Hooper ranch: "There was a time when we was on the lan'. They was a boundary to us then.... An' no we ain't clear no more.... We're crackin' up, Tom. There ain't no family now." (503).

Works Cited

Benson, Jackson J. *The True Adventures of John Steinbeck, Writer*. New York: Viking Press, 1984.

Carpenter, Fredric I., "The Philosophical Joads" *College English* 2, no. 4 (January 1941).

Con Davis, Robert, ed. *Twentieth Century Interpretations: The Grapes of Wrath*. Englewood Cliffs, NJ: Prentice-Hall, 1982.

Heavilin, Barbara A. John *Steinbeck's The Grapes of Wrath: A Reference Guide*. Westport, CT: Greenwood Press, 2002.

Railsback, Brian E. *Parallel Expeditions: Charles Darwin and the Art of John Steinbeck*. Moscow, Idaho: University of Idaho Press, 1995.

Critical Views

A book is published by one of our best novelists. It is greeted enthusiastically by critics as one of the most important books of our time. The American people like the book so much that it becomes one of the fastest-selling titles in American publishing history. That book, of course, is *The Grapes of Wrath*, by John Steinbeck, and we are glad to note that, according to our monthly tabulation of "current library favorites," it is the most popular title in our public libraries today. But there are some libraries where the book is not available despite the public demand for it. The Buffalo (N.Y.) Public Library has barred it because "vulgar words are employed by characters in the book." (There are vulgar words in Shakespeare and the Bible and *Tom Jones* and *Tristram Shandy* too, and for all we know maybe Buffalo bars them as well.) The public library in Kansas City has been ordered by the Board of Education to remove all copies of Steinbeck's "obscene" book from its shelves. The book is also banned in Kern County, California, where much of the action of the book takes place, and it is reported that the Associated Farmers (which is not a farmers' organization) hopes to forbid circulation of the book thruout the whole state. Librarians who have been told that they "ought to be ashamed to handle such a filthy book" may properly answer that of course we are ashamed, terribly ashamed, but not of the book. What we are ashamed of is that it could be written about our country, that it *had* to be written, that the conditions, the abuses, that it describes actually exist. *Factories in the Field*, a factual study by Carey McWilliams, ought to convince any skeptic that Steinbeck used more than nightmarish imagination in depicting the plight of the migratory farm workers. If the rumblings in Washington are any indication, "something is going to be done about it." You cannot muzzle a good book. You cannot keep the truth from being told.

As water implies baptism, the flood implies a new start—a re-Creation. Just as there was only one "tree" in the original Eden, there can be no "shame" in the discovery of the knowledge of good and evil in the new Eden. Steinbeck's Testament ends with a fusing of the significant actions of the Old and the New: the snake has been run over by a truck, anticipating the woman's heel; now there is only the "stuff people do," as Casy puts it (32), and the need for intellectualization has been obviated by direct experience. Rose of Sharon's action communicates an immediate redemption of a "chosen" people.

In these religious terms, therefore, the scene is almost devoid of sexuality—for all its sexual implications. Prurient interest remains in the eye of the beholder, and shame to him who thinks it evil. Sex exists here in its most abstracted, perfected sense; implicitly, however, it is within the understanding of the women, Ma and Rose of Sharon, who look "deep into each other" (618) before Rose of Sharon assents to Ma's request, unasked with words. What ensues is an almost philosophically justified use of sexual powers: right use of the body's intimate reproductive faculties to promote Life itself. Thus the ingredients for a possible dirty joke become the elements of an almost passive ritual. It is the reversing of, but also the concomitant of, the joyful flowing of life in the earlier scene of zestful copulation on the moving truck—with Connie and Rose of Sharon finding brief joy in their corner of the moving community; while Granma experiences her death struggle in another (306–07). Both the truck scene and the final tableau share a vitality so significant that both are accompanied by meaningful exchanges, of gifts paid for by losses: death (Granma, the baby) for life.

Finally, the final scene completes a turning-outward into society of energies that, in Greek or Faulknerian tragedy, might have turned into unproductive incestual frustrations. In the new familial system, older terminology is replaced by simpler concepts of "male" and "female" roles, and only the presence of external, social demands legitimizes what might otherwise have become sexual anarchy.

There is nothing remarkable in that a moral or religious progress, whose Christ-referents are ample, should end in an epiphany of sorts—miracle-plus-vision. The biblical, even medieval, instinct would have been to erect a shrine. Steinbeck constructs a kind of canopy over this final scene by rendering it as a tableau. The supposed improbability of this final act ignores the fact that the Joad family had long since been wrenched out of the conventional, traditional mores of viable family units. This is especially so after the dead child is set adrift without its sex even being determined. At this juncture, there has finally been a complete break with the past; and a transfer from the normal and specifically literal to the extraordinary and symbolic has been made possible. Thus a showing-forth ensues: a mixed action which shepherds and Magi might attend.

Therefore, Rose of Sharon becomes statuary, as worn mother and starving man fuse in a lasting composition. Steinbeck's endowment of the ordinarily human with exceptional qualities on extraordinary occasions is made possible by his exterior presentation during all other times— the result of his deliberately scientific, empirical approach to human nature, itself premised on the belief that humanity can never understand itself until it first understands the animal within the human. It is not, as Edmund Wilson phrased it in his classic missing-of-the-point, that Steinbeck tends "to present human life in animal terms," but that Steinbeck sees humanity as above the animal when it demonstrates the intelligence required to grasp its real situation and act accordingly—or when, driven by an evolutionary process to discover radical methods of survival as a species, it finds the instinctive understanding to make changes for the better. It is not, then, that Rose of Sharon "must offer her milk" to a starving stranger, as Wilson has it, out of an animal "loyalty to life itself." Rather, it is that people like the Joads finally understand what they will have to do for themselves if society should continue to fail to recognize their humanity; and Rose of Sharon's gesture is its admission. To say, as Wilson did, that "Mr. Steinbeck almost always in his fiction is dealing with the lower animals or with humans so rudimentary that they are almost on the animal level ..." is to display a peculiar distance from reality in the speaker himself.

Of course, Wilson was writing at the end of a decade—the thirties—when writers commonly described human beings out of a preconceived notion of human worth rather than by trying, as Steinbeck did, to decide what was truly human by observation. This approach by Steinbeck, when at his best, shows dehumanized human material straining upward towards its own ideal—precisely what occurs at the ending of *The Grapes of Wrath*. Negative interpretations such as Wilson's should not be allowed to obscure the validity of Steinbeck's ruthlessly honest (not "sentimental") questioning of the human condition: "What am I? What are the limitations inherent in my mode of existence?" Not only are Steinbeck's methods interestingly predictive of logical positivism and structuralism, but his approach to anthropology has become increasingly widespread as well. Rose of Sharon can be said to have pointed the way; extending the Mosaic parallels of the novel, we can say that with her act, mankind has been: to the mountain to see the Promised Land—rather than the "mirage" of the Joads' first sight of California. Thus she can be said to have acquired monumentality, the quality of significant statuary, in her final scene.

Again, Theodore Pollock correctly noted that the supposedly sentimental gesture under discussion occurs after the "human sacrifice" of Rose of Sharon's baby. But Rose of Sharon is openly abandoning, however intellectually and temporarily, conventional folk expectations about the attainment of futurity—the bearing of children to "carry on"— in order to establish futurity in societal, or "group," terms. Though Warren French footnotes Pollock's argument by drawing literal parallels of the scene "drought and downpour" with Eliot's *The Waste Land*, he does not take the argument far enough. Surely this dead infant, prophet of solidarity and "wrath," can also be paralleled with the same year-myth of "human sacrifice" that Eliot exploits, with all its suggestions of Nature-appeasement—and in a similar texture of spring's ironies. The exploration of Steinbeck's awareness and employment of myth has barely begun, in other words.

BRIAN E. RAILSBACK ON DARWINISM

A study of Charles Darwin and the art of John Steinbeck must, like any expedition through the novelist's life work, finally arrive at his masterpiece, *The Grapes of Wrath*. In no other book is Steinbeck's dramatization of Darwin's theory more clear; the novel resonates with the naturalist's ideas. Through Steinbeck's narrative technique, from the parts (i.e., the characters in the Joad chapters) to the whole (the intercalary chapters), we are presented with a holistic view of the migrant worker developed through Steinbeck's own inductive method. This epic novel demonstrates the range of Darwin's theory, including the essential aspects of evolution: the struggle for existence and the process of natural selection. The migrant workers move across the land as a species, uprooted from one niche and forced to gain a foothold in another. Their struggle is intensified by capitalism's perversion of natural competition, but this only makes the survivors that much tougher. Because of their inability to see the whole picture, the bankers and members of the Farmers Association diminish themselves by their oppressive tactics while the surviving migrant workers become increasingly tougher, more resourceful, and more sympathetic. Ultimately, seeing Darwin's ideas in *The Grapes of Wrath* enables us to perceive some hope for the Joads and others like them—here is Steinbeck's manifesto of progress, based on biological laws rather than political ideology. Despite the dismal scene that concludes the book, we come to a better understanding of what Ma Joad already knows, that "the people" will keep on coming.

(...)

A Darwinian interpretation of *The Grapes of Wrath* reveals the novel's most terrible irony: the owners' perversion of the natural process only hastens their own destruction. In states such as Oklahoma, the bank—the "monster"—must be fed at the expense of the tenant system, thus losing something precious: "The man who is more than his chemistry ... that man who is more than his elements knows the land that is more than its analysis" (126). And the tenacity of these people, their potential, is drawn to another land. The Farmers Association of California sends out handbills to attract a surplus of labor, intensifying the competition for jobs so that the migrant laborers will work for almost nothing. But the owners are unconscious of the other part of the equation, that increased competition only toughens the survivors, as Darwin notes: "In the survival of favored individuals and races, during the constantly recurrent Struggle for Existence, we see a powerful and everacting form of Selection" (Appleman, *Origin* 115). The novel's omniscient narrator recalls "the little screaming fact" evident throughout history, of which the owners remain ignorant: "repression works only to strengthen and knit the repressed" (*Grapes* 262).

Steinbeck recognizes the untenable position of the owners in California. "Having built the repressive attitude toward the labor they need to survive, the directors were terrified of the things they have created" (*Gypsies* 36). As the economic system blindly pushes people out of the plains states and just as blindly entices them to California with the intention of inhumane exploitation, it proves a system of men who fail to see the whole. Often the owners win, and some workers are hungry enough to betray their own kind, such as the migrants hired to move in and break up the dance at Weedpatch. But at the end of chapter 19, the omniscient voice describes how in their suffering people come together, as the migrants gather coins to bury a dead infant; soon they will see beyond themselves and the illusion of their religion. "And the association of owners knew that some day the praying would stop. And there's the end" (*Graves* 263).

(...)

In a work so full of apparently hopeless suffering, the Darwinian view of *The Grapes of Wrath* explains why characters such as Ma or Tom have a sense of victory. The processes of competition and natural selection, artificially heightened by narrow-minded landowners, create a new race with strong blood—a race that can adapt and fight in a way the old one could not. Endowed with a closeness to the land and an increasing sympathy, this new race represents a human being far superior to the old "I" savage. Because of the struggle, people like the Joads become better human beings, cooperating with each other in every crisis. "There is a gradual improvement in the treatment of man by man," Steinbeck wrote in a letter for the *Monthly Record* (a magazine for the Connecticut state prison system) during the period in which *The Grapes of Wrath* was being written. "There are little spots of kindness that burn up like fire and light the whole thing up. But I guess the reason they are so bright is that there are so few of them. However, the ones that do burn up seem to push us ahead a little" (3). Thus, even when famished and facing death herself, Rose of Sharon begins to see past her own selfishness and offers her breast to a starving man. She has reason to smile mysteriously, understanding something larger and greater than her oppressors will ever know.

MALCOLM COWLEY ON STEINBECK'S "FIGHT AGAINST INTOLERABLE WRONGS"

While keeping our eyes on the cataclysms in Europe and Asia, we have lost sight of a tragedy nearer home. A hundred thousand rural households have been uprooted from the soil, robbed of their possessions—though by strictly legal methods—and turned out on the highways. Friendless, homeless and therefore voteless, with fewer rights than medieval serfs, they have wandered in search of a few days' work at miserable wages—not in Spain or the Yangtze Valley, but among the vineyards and orchards of California, in a setting too commonplace for a color story in the Sunday papers. Their migrations have been described only in a long poem and a novel. The poem is "Land of the Free," by Archibald MacLeish, published last year with terrifying photographs by the Resettlement Administration. The novel, which has just appeared, is John Steinbeck's longest and angriest and most impressive work.

The Grapes of Wrath begins with Tom Joad's homecoming. After being released from the Oklahoma State Penitentiary, where he has served four years of a seven-year sentence for homicide, he sets out for his father's little farm in the bottom lands near Sallisaw. He reaches the house to find that it is empty, the windows broken, the well filled in and even the dooryard planted with cotton. Muley Graves, a neighbor, comes past in the dusk and tells him what has happened. It is a scene that I can't forget: the men sitting back on their haunches, drawing figures with a stick in the dust; a half-starved cat watching from the doorstep; and around them the silence of a mile-long cottonfield. Muley says that all the tenant farmers have been evicted from their land—"tractored off" is the term he uses. Groups of twenty and thirty farms are being thrown together and the whole area cultivated by one man with a caterpillar tractor. Most of the families are moving to California, on the rumor that work can be found there. Tom's people are staying temporarily with his Uncle John, eight miles away, but they will soon be leaving. Of this whole farming community, no one is left but stubborn Muley Graves, hiding from the sheriff's men, haunting empty houses and "jus' wanderin' aroun'," he says, "like an of graveyard ghos'."

Next morning Tom rejoins his family—just in time, for the uncle too has been ordered to leave his farm. The whole family of twelve is starting for California. Their last day at home is another fine scene in which you realize, little by little, that not only a family but a whole culture is being uprooted—a primitive culture, it is true, but complete in its fashion, with its history, its legends of Indian fighting, its songs and jokes, its religious practices, its habits of work and courtship; even the killing of two hogs is a ritual.

With the hogs salted down and packed in the broken-down truck among the bedclothes, the Joads start westward on U.S. Highway 66. They are part of an endless caravan—trucks, trailers, battered sedans, touring cars rescued from the junkyard, all of them overloaded with children and household plunder, all wheezing, pounding and screeching toward California. There are deaths on the road—Gramps is the first to go—but there is not much time for mourning. A greater tragedy than death is a burned-out bearing, repaired after efforts that Steinbeck describes as if he were singing the exploits of heroes at the siege of Troy. Then, after a last wild ride through the desert—Tom driving, Rose of Sharon and her husband making love and Gramma dying under the same tarpaulin—the Joads cross the pass at Tehachapi and see before them the promised land, the grainfields golden in the morning.

The second half of the novel, dealing with their adventures in the Valley of California, is still good but somewhat less impressive. Until that moment the Joads have been moving steadily toward their goal. Now they discover that it is not their goal after all; they must still move on, but no longer in one direction—they are harried by vigilantes, recruited as peach pickers, driven out again by a strike; they don't know where to go. Instead of being just people, as they were at home, they hear themselves called Okies—"and that means you're scum," they tell each other bewilderedly. "Don't mean nothing itself, it's the way they say it." The story begins to suffer a little from their bewilderment and lack of direction.

At this point one begins to notice other faults. Interspersed among the chapters that tell what happened to the Joads, there have been other chapters dealing with the general plight of the migrants. The first half dozen of these interludes have not only broadened the scope of the novel but have been effective in themselves, sorrowful, bitter, intensely moving. But after the Joads reach California, the interludes are spoken in a shriller voice. The author now has a thesis—that the migrants will unite and overthrow their oppressors—and he wants to argue, as if he weren't quite sure of it himself. His thesis is also embodied in one of the characters: Jim Casy, a preacher who loses his faith but unfortunately for the reader can't stop preaching. In the second half of the novel, Casy becomes a Christ-like labor leader and is killed by vigilantes. The book ends with an episode that is a mixture of allegory and melodrama. Rose of Sharon, after her baby is born dead, saves a man from starvation by suckling him at her breast—as if to symbolize the fruitfulness of these people and the bond that unites them in misfortune.

Yet one soon forgets the faults of the story. What one remembers most of all is Steinbeck's sympathy for the migrants—not pity, for that would mean he was putting himself above them; not love, for that would blind him to their faults, but rather a deep fellow feeling. It makes him notice everything that sets them apart from the rest of the world and sets one migrant apart from all the others. In the Joad family, everyone from Gramma—"Full a' piss an' vinegar," as he says of himself—down to the two brats, Ruthie and Winfield, is a distinct and living person. And the story is living too—it has the force of the headlong anger that drives ahead from the first chapter to the last, as if the whole six hundred pages were written without stopping. The author and the reader are swept along together. I can't agree with those critics who say that *The Grapes of Wrath* is the greatest novel of the last ten years; for example, it doesn't rank with the best of Hemingway or Dos Passos. But it belongs very high in the category of the great angry books like *Uncle Tom's Cabin* that have roused a people to fight against intolerable wrongs.

FREDERIC I. CARPENTER ON THE NOVEL AND AMERICAN TRANSCENDENTALISM

"This is the beginning," he writes, "from 'I' to 'we.'" This is the beginning, that is, of reconstruction. When the old society has been split and the Protestant individuals wander aimlessly about, some new nucleus must be found, or chaos and nihilism will follow. "In the night one family camps in a ditch and another family pulls in and the tents come out. The two men squat on their hams and the women and children listen. Here is the node." Here is the new nucleus. "And from this first 'we,' there grows a still more dangerous thing: 'I have a little food' plus 'I have none.' If from this problem the sum is 'We have a little food,' the thing is on its way, the movement has direction." A new social group is forming, based on the word "en masse." But here is no socialism imposed from above; here is a natural grouping of simple separate persons.

By virtue of his wholehearted participation in this new group the individual may become greater than himself. Some men, of course, will remain mere individuals, but in every group there must be leaders, or "representative men." A poet gives expression to the group idea, or a preacher organizes it. After Jim Casy's death, Tom is chosen to lead. Ma explains: "They's some folks that's just theirself, an' nothin' more. There's Al [for instance] he's jus' a young fella after a girl. You wasn't never like that, Tom." Because he has been an individualist, but through the influence of Casy and of his group idea has become more than himself, Tom becomes "a leader of the people." But his strength derives from his increased sense of participation in the group.

From Jim Casy, and eventually from the thought of Americans like Whitman, Tom Joad has inherited this idea. At the end of the book he sums it up, recalling how Casy "went out in the wilderness to find his own soul, and he found he didn't have no soul that was his'n. Says he foun' he jus' got a little piece of a great big soul. Says a wilderness ain't no good 'cause his little piece of a soul wasn't no good 'less it was with the rest, an' was whole." Unlike Emerson, who had said goodbye to the proud world, these latter-day Americans must live in the midst of it. "I know now," concludes Tom, "a fella ain't no good alone."

(...)

The fundamental idea of *The Grapes of Wrath* is that of

American transcendentalism: "Maybe all men got one big soul every'body's a part of." From this idea it follows that every individual will trust those instincts which he shares with all men, even when these conflict with the teachings of orthodox religion and of existing society. But his self-reliance will not merely seek individual freedom, as did Emerson. It will rather seek social freedom or mass democracy, as did Whitman. If this mass democracy leads to the abandonment of genteel taboos and to the modification of some traditional ideas of morality, that is inevitable. But whatever happens, the American will act to realize his ideals. He will seek to make himself whole—i.e., to join himself to other men by means of purposeful actions for some goal beyond himself.

(...)

For the first time in history, *The Grapes of Wrath* brings together and makes real three great skeins of American thought. It begins with the transcendental oversoul, Emerson's faith in the common man, and his Protestant self-reliance. To this it joins Whitman's religion of the love of all men and his mass democracy. And it combines these mystical and poetic ideas with the realistic philosophy of pragmatism and its emphasis on effective action. From this it develops a new kind of Christianity—not otherworldly and passive, but earthly and active. And Oklahoma Jim Casy and the Joads think and do all these philosophical things.

J. PAUL HUNTER ON THE BIBLE AND THE NOVEL AND THE CHARACTERS OF JIM CASY AND ROSE OF SHARON

Casy's role is central to the structure of *The Grapes of Wrath*, for in him the narrative structure and the thematic structure are united. This role is best seen when set against the Biblical background which informs both types of structure in the novel.

Peter Lisca has noted that the novel reflects the three-part division of the Old Testament exodus account (captivity, journey, promised land), but that the "parallel is not worked out in detail." Actually, the lack of detailed parallel seems to be deliberate, for Steinbeck is reflecting a broader background of which the exodus story is only a part.

Steinbeck makes the incidents in his novel suggest a wide range of old and New Testament stories. As the twelve Joads (corresponding to the twelve tribes of Israel) embark on their journey (leaving the old order behind), they mount the truck in ark fashion, two by two:

> ... the rest swarmed up on top of the load, Connie and Rose of Sharon, Pa and Uncle John, Ruthie and Winfield, Tom and the preacher. Noah stood on the ground looking up at the great load of them sitting on top of the truck.

Grampa (like Lot's wife) is unable to cope with the thought of a new life, and his wistful look at the past brings his death—a parallel emphasized by the scripture verse (quoting Lot) which Tom picks out to bury with Grampa. Uncle John (like Ananias) withholds money from the common fund, in order to satisfy his selfish desires. The list could be lengthened extensively, and many allusions are as isolated and apparently unrelated to the context as the ones cited here. Looked at in one way, these allusions seem patternless, for they refer to widely separated sections of Biblical history. However, the frequency of allusion suggests the basic similarity between the plight of the Joads and that of the Hebrew people. Rather than paralleling a single section of Biblical history, the novel reflects the broader history of the chosen people from their physical bondage to their spiritual release by means of a messiah.

If the reader approaches *The Grapes of Wrath* searching for too exact a parallel, he will be disappointed, for just when it seems as if a one-to-one ratio exists, Steinbeck breaks the pattern. Tom, for example, is a Moses-type leader of his people as they journey toward the promised land. Like Moses, he has killed a man and has been away for a time before rejoining his people and becoming their leader. Like Moses, he has a younger brother (Aaron-Al) who serves as a vehicle for the leader (spokesman-truck driver). And shortly before reaching the destination, he hears and rejects the evil reports of those who have visited the land (Hebrew "spies"—Oklahomans going back). But soon the parallel ends. Carried out carefully at the beginning, it does not seem to exist once the journey is completed. Granma, not Tom, dies just before the new land is reached, and Tom remains the leader of the people until finally (and here a different parallel is suggested) he becomes a disciple of Casy's gospel. This, in the miniature of one character, is what continually happens in *The Grapes of Wrath*. The scene changes, the parallel breaks; and gradually the context shifts from a basically Old Testament one to a New Testament one.

Steinbeck makes his allusions suggestive, rather than exhaustive, and he implies certain parallels without calling for too rigid an allegorical reading. In *East of Eden* Steinbeck also uses the method of suggestive allusion, and Adam's sons are not named Cain and Abel, but Caleb and Aaron (note the initials game again). This is no mere puzzle or covering of tracks, for the method serves to nullify too literal a reading, while at the same time drawing in a whole new range of suggestions. Instead of only Abel, the reader is asked to recall also the Biblical characteristics of another No. 2 brother. In *The Grapes of Wrath*, the method gives Steinbeck the freedom to skirt the particularly vexing time problem, for in the background myth the changes in the Hebrew people take place over centuries, while similar ideological changes in Steinbeck's characters occur within one year. In effect, Steinbeck collapses several hundred years of Hebrew history into the single year of his story; the entire history of man (according to the Judeo-Christian tradition) is reflected in the long hungry summer of one persecuted family.

This span of centuries is focused in Casy, whose ideas bridge the gap from Old to New Testament (according to the Christian concept of Biblical thought as developmental). Parallels between the life of Jim Casy and the messiah whose initials he bears are plentiful. He embarks upon his mission after a long period of meditation in the wilderness; he corrects the old ideas of religion and justice; he selflessly sacrifices himself for his cause, and when he dies he tells his persecutors, "'You don' know what you're a-doin'.'" Less obvious perhaps, but equally important, is the role of the old Casy, before his wilderness experience, for he must ultimately be considered in messianic rather than Christological terms. Casy had been a typical hell-and-damnation evangelist who emphasized the rigidity of the old moral law and who considered himself ultimately doomed because human frailty prevented his achieving the purity demanded by the law. His conversion to a social gospel represents a movement from Old Testament to New Testament thought, an expanded horizon of responsibility. The annunciation of Casy's message and mission sets the ideological direction of the novel before the journey begins (just as the messiah concept influences Jewish thought for centuries before New Testament times), but only gradually does Casy make an impression upon a people (Jew-Joads) used to living under the old dispensation. Over Route 66 he rides quietly—a guest, a thirteenth—and only as time passes does the new idea blossom and the new order emerge; and the outsider—the thirteenth—becomes spiritual leader of a people to whom he had been a convention, a grace before meals.

Steinbeck's canvas is, on the surface, a painting of broad modern strokes, but its scenes are sketched along the outlines of the Judeo-Christian myth, a sort of polyptych depicting man's sojourn in a hostile world. The background is often faded, sometimes erased, and occasionally distorted, but structurally and ideologically it provides depth for Steinbeck's modern microcosm. In *The Grapes of Wrath* the background ideology becomes secularized and transcendentalized, but the direction of thought is still recognizable: a widening of concern. After the dispersion, there is still a saving remnant whose compassion begins to extend beyond its own familial or tribal group.

Steinbeck's method is perhaps not uniformly successful, and in some work done in this manner (such as *East of Eden* and

Burning Bright) the fusion of the particular and the mythic seems, if not less perfectly conceived, less carefully wrought. But in *The Grapes of Wrath* the modern and mythic are peculiarly at one, and the story of a family which, in the values of its contemporary society, is hardly worth a jot, is invested with meaning when viewed against a history of enduring significance.

(...)

Rose of Sharon's sacrificial act represents the final breakdown of old attitudes, and climaxes the novel's thematic movement. The final bastion of the old order, Rose of Sharon had been the most selfish of the remaining Joads; her concern had never extended beyond herself and her immediate family (Connie and the expected child). In giving life to the stranger (symbolically, she gives body and wine: Song of Songs 7:7—"Thy breasts [are like] to clusters of grapes"), she accepts the larger vision of Jim Casy, and her commitment fulfills the terms of salvation according to Casy's plan. In their hesitancy and confusion in the old times, the Joads had been powerless to change their fate. Unlike the turtle who dragged through the dust and planted the seeds of the future, they had drawn figures in the dust impotently with sticks. Now, however, they too are purposeful and share the secret of giving life.

The Biblical myth informs the final scene through a cluster of symbols which emphasize the change and affirm the new order. As the Joads hover in the one dry place in their world—a barn—the Bible's three major symbols of a purified order are suggested: the Old Testament deluge, the New Testament stable, and the continuing ritual of communion. In the fusion of the three, the novel's mythic background, ideological progression, and modern setting are brought together; Mt. Ararat, Bethlehem, and California are collapsed into a single unit of time, and life is affirmed in a massive symbol of regeneration.

The novel's final picture—a still life of Rose of Sharon holding the old man—combines the horror with the hope. Its imitation of the madonna and child (one face mysteriously smiling; the other wasted, and with wide, frightened eyes) is a grotesque one, for it reflects a grotesque world without painless answers, a world where men are hit by axe handles and children suffer from skitters. Steinbeck does not promise Paradise for the Joads. Their wildest dreams image not golden streets, but indoor plumbing. Dams will continue to break—babies will continue to be stillborn. But the people will go on: "this is the beginning—from 'I' to 'we.'" The grapes of wrath have ripened, and in trampling out the vintage the Dispossessed have committed themselves (like Casy) to die to make men free. In despair they learn the lesson; in wrath they share the rich red wine of hope.

NELLIE Y. MCKAY ON SOCIAL CHANGE, THE REDEFINITION OF FAMILY, AND MOTHERHOOD

There is no question that Steinbeck had, as Howard Levant stresses, "profound respect" and "serious intentions" for the materials in *The Grapes of Wrath*. His sympathies are with a group of people who, though politically and economically unaggressive by other traditional American standards, represented an important core in the national life.[29] His portrayal of the misfortunes and downfall of this family constitutes a severe critique of a modern economic system that not only devalues human lives on the basis of class but, in so doing, that violates the principles of the relationship between hard work and reward and the sanctity of white family life on which the country was founded. In light of the brutal social and economic changes, and the disruptions of white family stability, there is no doubt that Steinbeck saw strong women from traditional working-class backgrounds as instrumental in a more humane transformation of the social structure. Of necessity, women are essential to any novel in which the conventional family plays a significant role. Here, he gives the same significance to the destruction of a family-centered way of life that one group had shaped and perpetuated for generations as he does to the economic factors that precipitated such a dire situation. Furthermore, through female characters in *The Grapes of Wrath*, Steinbeck's sensitivities to the values of female sensibilities demonstrate a point of view that supports the idea of humanitarian, large-scale changes that would make America, as a nation, more responsive to larger social needs.

In this respect, in spite of the grim reality of the lives of the Joads and their neighbors, *The Grapes of Wrath* is optimistic in favor of massive social change. We can trace this optimism from the beginning of the book, in which, unlike traditional plots of the naturalistic novels of its day, events unfold through the consciousness of the characters in such a way as to permit them to envision themselves exercising free will and exerting influence on their social world. In addition, as a result of his economic politics, Steinbeck reinforces the idea that the situation is not the dilemma of an isolated family, but of an entire group of people of a particular class. If sufficiently politicized, they can and will act. The novel chronicles the misfortunes and political education of the Joad family, but they represent the group from which they come, and share the feelings of their like-others. For example, also at the beginning, an unnamed farmer, recognizing his individual impotence in the face of capitalism and the technological monster, protests: "We've got a bad thing made by man, and by God that's something *we* can change" (52—italics mine). While neither he nor his fellow farmers can comprehend the full meaning of that statement at the time, the end of the novel suggests that those who survive will come to realize that group action can have an effect on the monstrous ideology that threatens their existence. But first they must survive; and the women are at the center of making that survival possible.

(...)

In Steinbeck's vision of a different and more humane society than capitalistic greed spawned, he also believed that efforts like Ma Joad's, to hold the family together in the way she always knew it (individualism as a viable social dynamic), were doomed to failure. Although she is unconscious of it at the time, her initial embrace of Casy is a step toward a redefinition of family, and, by the time the Joads arrive in California, other developments have already changed the situation. Both Grampa and Granma are dead. Soon after, son Noah, feeling himself a burden on the meager resources at hand, wanders away. In addition, Casy is murdered for union activities; Al, whose mechanical genius was invaluable during the trip, is ready to marry and leave; Connie, Rose of Sharon's husband, deserts, and her baby is stillborn; and Tom, in an effort to avenge Casy's death, becomes a fugitive from the law and decides to become a union organizer, to carry on Casy's work. Through these events, first Tom, and then Ma, especially through Tom's final conversation with her, achieve an education in the politics of class oppression, and realize that the system that diminishes one family to the point of its physical and moral disintegration can only be destroyed through the cooperative efforts of those of the oppressed group. "Use' ta be the fambly was fust. It ain't so now. It's anybody," Ma is forced to admit toward the end of the novel (606).

But, although the structure of the traditional family changes to meet the needs of a changing society, in this novel at least, Steinbeck sees "happy-wife-and-motherdom" as the central role for women, even for those with other significant contributions to make to the world at large. Ma Joad's education in the possibilities of class action do not extend to an awareness of women's lives and identities beyond the domestic sphere, other than that which has a direct relationship on the survival of the family. The conclusion of the novel revises the boundaries of that family. In this scene, unable physically to supply milk from her own breasts to save the old man's life, she initiates her daughter into the sisterhood of "mothering the world," of perpetuating what Nancy Chodorow calls "The Reproduction of Mothering." Ma Joad is the epitome of the Earth Mother. Critics note that Steinbeck need give her no first name, for she is the paradigmatic mother, and this is the single interest of her life. The seventeenth- and eighteenth-century metaphor of the fecund, virgin American land (women) gives way to that of the middle-aged mother (earth), "thick with child-bearing and work," but Steinbeck holds onto the stereotypical parallels between woman and nature. In our typical understanding of that word, Ma may not be happy in her role, but "her face ... [is] controlled and kindly" and she fully accepts her place. Having "experienced all possible tragedy and ... mounted pain and suffering like steps into a high calm," she fulfills her highest calling in the realm of wife and motherdom.

Note

29. See Kolodny, pp. 26–28 for an account of the high regard men like Thomas Jefferson had for the small farmer. In spite of the benefits of large-scale farming, he advocated the independent, family-size farm, and believed that those who tilled the earth gained "substantial and genuine virtue."

Warren French on Steinbeck and Modernism

There is still so little agreement about the nature of Modernism—despite general agreement about its coming and going—that I have had to place my remarks about John Steinbeck against a background of what I must remind you is purely my personal conception of what the Modernist sensibility "is" or "was." Clearly this concept must have some relationship to John Steinbeck, because his whole career is contained within this period; but what was this relationship? In my tribute to Marston LaFrance in the *Steinbeck Quarterly*, Winter 1976, I outlined my answer to this question: "Certainly there would [be a place it a study of the Modernist period] for attention to John Steinbeck, because the 'ironic vision' that LaFrance attributes to Crane is fundamentally what Steinbeck was attempting to describe through his long preoccupation with 'non-teleological thinking' and Steinbeck's fiction was marked by this intrinsically ironic outlook from the earliest known specimens (like "Saint Katy the Virgin") to *Of Mice and Men*. The quality disappeared only after whatever Pauline vision occurred on Steinbeck's private road to Damascus caused him to re-draft the work that became *The Grapes of Wrath*." I do hope that readers may have found this pronouncement intriguingly or infuriatingly inadequate; surely it needs development, and I think that this bicentennial seminar provides the opportunity that I have wanted to expand my perception of Steinbeck's relationship to our national literature and the dominant literary trend of his age.

(...)

"The meanness and the plannings and the discontent and the ache for attention": these are the visible symbols of the characteristic alienation of the Modernist period. When shall they be gone from our faces and by what magic removed? For the characters in Steinbeck's blackest work, only in death! Every evidence indicates that Steinbeck intended the book once called *L'Affaire Lettuceberg*, then retitled *The Grapes of Wrath*, to follow up and confirm the example of *In Dubious Battle* and *Of Mice and Men*; but about halfway through the project he wrote to his publishers that although the book was finished, "it is a bad book and I must get rid of it," because "My whole work drive has been aimed at making people understand each other and then I deliberately write this book, the aim of which is to cause hatred through partial understanding" (Lisca, *The Wide World of John Steinbeck*, p. 147). Interestingly, he objected to writing satire, because it "restricted" the picture, what Kierkegaard described as "abstracting" from the personal ego. Steinbeck had rejected the Modernist double vision with its defeatist implications. He was never to return to this vision, although his early novels, which established his reputation, are almost models of the alienated Modernist sensibility, displaying (to take just one example, in *Tortilla Flat*) all the characteristics that Maurice Beebe lists—the formalistic structure and mythological order borrowed from the *Morte d'Arthur* and the detachment and concern with composition exemplified by his self-conscious explanations of the structuring of the work, as well as—surely as powerfully as possible—the effort to free one's self from the middle class that Lionel Trilling had found "the chief intention of all modern literature." Although this Modernist sensibility was to continue to dominate our literature until the early 1970s, Steinbeck had abandoned it by 1938 before the publication of what remains his most monumental work.

There is not time on this occasion to describe fully what came afterwards, where Steinbeck moved from Modernism; but the question is of such large importance to the development of our literature that I feel obliged to add to this discussion of Steinbeck and Modernism a postscript outlining the viewpoints that dominated his subsequent works and especially my concept of an important cause for the decline in the power of his work that it is widely agreed occurred after World War II.

What Steinbeck did in reshaping *L'Affaire Lettuceberg* into *The Grapes of Wrath* was to transcend the ironic detachment of Modernism with a new affirmative conception of individual regeneration. Elsewhere I have argued that the Joad story in the novel portrays "the education of the heart." The Joads have failed to achieve full self-realization, not because of their persecution by a soulless society, but because they themselves have had the expansion of their consciousness limited by the reductivist concept of "family": "Use'ta be the fambly was fust," Ma Joad tells a neighbor at the final turning-point of the story, "It ain't so now. It's anybody." Under the power of preacher Casy's example, the Joads have come to realize that "it's all men an' all women we love." Although the term would not have been used then, *The Grapes of Wrath* is a fiction of consciousness-raising."

Stuart L. Burns on the Symbol of the Turtle

Critics generally agree that the parable of the turtle presented in chapter three of *The Grapes of Wrath* foreshadows and parallels the adventures of the Joad family. Almost as unanimously, they agree that the concluding scene of the novel dramatizes Steinbeck's theme that, as Ma Joad states it, "the people ... go on."[1] To be sure, there has been considerable controversy about the propriety of the conclusion—whether it is dramatic, poignant, sentimental, vulgar, or obscene. But most scholars agree about its meaning. I am inclined to believe that the critics have correctly assessed Steinbeck's intent in both instances. But whatever his intent, this is not what he accomplished. For the affirmative parable of the turtle provides a contrast, not a parallel, to the tragic story of the Joads.

(...)

There are certain similarities between the turtle and the Joads, of course: it is heading southwest, as will they; the highway (but not the same highway) is a formidable obstacle to both; and the overloaded Hudson certainly travels at a turtle's pace. But consider the very real and thematically more meaningful distinctions. The turtle has an instinctive sense of purpose and direction; it turns "aside for nothing" (20). And while one cannot know for certain where the turtle is going or what it intends to do when it gets there, the context clearly implies that it will get there and accomplish whatever it has instinctively set out to do. The Joads, on the other hand, head southwest due to circumstances beyond their control. They have at first no desire to move at all, and throughout a nostalgia for the Oklahoma farm they were forced to leave. And only an unflagging optimist would connect their concluding situation, or for that matter their future prospects, with any concrete achievement. But perhaps the most significant distinction between the turtle and the Joads is that, whereas the former plays a fertilizing role to the "sleeping life waiting to be dispersed" (20), the life that Rosasharn carries is delivered premature and stillborn. Twelve Joads spanning three generations (thirteen spanning four if one counts the unborn baby) begin the journey; although ten presumably survive, only six are together at the end. The emphasis is on attrition, not continuance.

If one examines subsequent passages in the novel where the turtle is alluded to, the difference between the positive thrust of the parable and the negative thrust of the narrative becomes even clearer. Two characters, Tom Joad and Jim Casy, are specifically associated with the turtle. Tom picks it up and carries it with him for a while (to the northeast, opposite the turtle's intended direction); and Casy's physical description is suggestive of a turtle. He has a "long head, bony, tight of skin, and set on a neck as stringy and muscular as a celery stalk." His "heavy ... protruding" eyeballs with lids stretched to cover them" (25) are decidedly reptilian. That Tom and Casy should be closely associated with the turtle is appropriate inasmuch as, of the thirteen people who trek west in the Hudson, these two do develop a sense of purpose and direction akin to the turtle's. But the analogy has its limits. The turtle survives its encounter with the hostile forces of civilization. Indeed, the truck which swerves to hit it actually flips it across the highway, aiding it in this hazardous crossing. Casy, who has no protective shell into which he can withdraw his head, has it crushed by a pick handle wielded by the leader of the mob at the Hooper ranch. And while Tom survives on this occasion, his future—a hunted ex-convict turned labor agitator—bodes nothing but ill. The text suggests that the turtle will survive because it expends its energies totally in its self-interest; Casy dies because he devotes his energies to helping others.

This distinction between self-interest and humanitarianism is further illustrated in another brief scene in which Granma is associated with the turtle. The red ant which crawls "over the folds of loose skin on her neck" (286) while she is dying recalls the ant the turtle crushes inside its shell (20). But, whereas the turtle reacts savagely and effectively, Granma is able to do no more than feebly scratch her face. To be sure, Ma Joad crushes the ant "between thumb and forefinger" (286), in a gesture reminiscent of the turtle's action. But this only reinforces the point that, as Tom Joad states later, "a fella ain't no good alone" (570).

The point of difference can be illustrated in terms of one other dominant motif in the novel. Animals are indifferent to and can survive the damage done by machines. The Joads' house cat turns wild and remains on the tenant farm. The turtle is actually aided by the truck whose driver tries to kill it. The Joads, by contrast, are first displaced by machines, then rendered helplessly dependent on the Hudson to get them to California. And while an occasional person like Muley Graves may exist as does the house cat,[2] there is no character whose pattern of behavior is suggestive of the indomitable will of the turtle. If there is one character in the novel who seems most likely to survive and make a decent life for himself, that would have to be Al Joad. But Al will succeed only if he has the callousness to wrest himself free of family dependence on him—he is the only remaining member who can drive the truck—and get himself that dreamed-of job in a garage. That is to say, he can survive by joining the side that owns and runs the machines; by acting, in short, a little less like a decent human being and a little more like the turtle.

Notes

1. *The Grapes of Wrath* (New York: The Viking Press, 1958), p. 383. All subsequent quotations from the novel will refer to this edition, and page numbers will be included in the text.

2. But, even here, his name has a connotation negative to the idea of survival.

EDWIN T. BOWDEN ON THE OKIES AND ISOLATION

John Steinbeck's *The Grapes of Wrath* marked another step for the modern age when it took up the question of isolation not only for a few particular characters but for a whole people, and considered it in a novel that belongs in many respects with *The Rise of Silas Lapham* and *Winesburg, Ohio* in a group of the grotesque and the commonplace. It is a novel of the agricultural depression of the 1930's and that memory of the folly and failure of man, the dust bowl. Yet it is a novel not about conditions but about people, the commonplace people of a Howells—even though Howells would have been shocked at the novel itself. Steinbeck's despair and indignation are too great for a Howells, and his characters are far from the familiar society of a Howells. Like Anderson and Faulkner, in contrast to Howells, he even questions the assumption of free will in the individual. Yet his people must meet the commonplace problems of life—food, shelter, clothing, medical aid—and their desires are the desires of the commonplace man—happiness, love, family unity, self-respect, a feeling of belonging. They are the common men of the new century. In another sense, however, the novel is not about commonplace man but about a special, often grotesque group of men, the Okies, the dispossessed of the dust bowl, the new itinerant farm laborers of California. And one of the successes of the novel is the manner in which it conveys simultaneously the impression, almost an epic impression, of a whole people migrating westward and the familiar view of one particular family facing its particular problems. The Joad family, even though unique, is a part of a whole people; and this novel, unlike most of the novels of the previous century, is as much about a people as it is about a few central people. In the midst of a blighting depression the concern for the individual begins to give way to the concern for the people, even though paradoxically it was this novel, probably more than any other, that convinced America that the group scornfully called Okies was after all made up of familiar and commonplace individuals.

(...)

In *The Grapes of Wrath* there are plenty of "others" to hold the Okies in isolation. Sometimes they act out of the brutality and hatred born of fear, as the deputies who destroy the Hooverville camps. Sometimes they act out of selfishness and desire for personal gain, as the orchard owners who break up the strike against starvation wages. But whatever the immediate motivation, all deny the humanity and the individual worth of the Okies. The service-station boy on Route 66, even though he takes no direct action, is representative in his thought:

"Well, you and me got sense. Them goddamn Okies got no sense and no feeling. They ain't human. A human being wouldn't live like they do. A human being couldn't stand it to be so dirty and miserable. They ain't a hell of a lot better than gorillas." [301]

Against the isolation imposed by such an attitude the Okies see no recourse beyond banding together more solidly in mutual aid and understanding. If at times they believe too much in mere organization for its own sake—defended in part by the assumption of the common nature of man—their longing can be understood in terms of the times and their situation. The "others," after all, have banded together, not out of a desire to serve their common humanity, but rather out of a selfish desire to exploit the unorganized. For the individual to fight back alone may be heroic, but it is fatal. As an extreme case of the isolated individual against the world the story of Pretty Boy Floyd is mentioned again and again; " 'They run him like a coyote, an' him a-snappin' an' a-snarlin', mean as a lobo.' " [103] But the Okies of this novel do not turn into that sort of outlaw. Driven out of the home and the society they once knew, wandering in isolation among those who cannot even accept them as members of a common humanity, they can only turn to each other for help and understanding and love. And there, bound together by their mutual plight, forced into a recognition of the humanity of others, they can lose the loneliness that their isolation threatens.

For all its modern setting, then, for all its time of unusual conditions and its interest in a whole people as well as in the individual, *The Grapes of Wrath* is still clearly in the tradition of the American concern in fiction for the problem of isolation. It has simply broadened the theme, in keeping with the sociological interest imposed by the century, to include a group rather than person. The Joads must each meet the problem of alienation in his own way, yet behind the individual there is always the family, and behind the family there is always the whole tribe of migrants, each individual and each group of which must meet the problem too. And the answer for all is still the old answer for the individual: the loss of self in concern and love for others. If man can lose his exclusively egocentric and selfish interest to turn outward to others, he need not fear loneliness or spiritual isolation. For this century the mechanics of the solution may be somewhat different from those of earlier days. Man can no longer simply turn to humanity—desirable as that ideal is—but must belong to some form of group to which to turn. Even then the answer is not simple, for the group may itself be devoted to inhumane ends, as is the organization of farmers and canners in this novel. So man must turn to the group, and the group must turn to humanity itself. The individual is no longer in complete control of his own end, as Anderson and Faulkner imply, but must depend upon others as well as himself. But the others, as *The Grapes of Wrath* insists so successfully, are themselves individuals. And if the individuals of this modern complex, organized world would always keep faith with their common humanity in their necessary organization, the ideal world in which there is no isolation and no loneliness would be achieved. The goal may never be reached—and the fiction of this century is hardly optimistic— but man in the meanwhile has an immediate answer that will serve his needs and will eventually help the step toward the ideal. When man can turn out of himself to others he can escape spiritual loneliness, whatever his isolation may be.

MARY ELLEN CALDWELL ON CHAPTER 15 AND THE EPITOME OF *THE GRAPES OF WRATH*

Chapter 15 is placed in the center of the book, by chapter count, not by page count. It is neither a purely intercalary chapter as the others are nor is it a part of the Joad narrative. It is an epitome of the whole book, having its own narrative paragraphs and intercalary paragraphs.

Steinbeck starts out with a panoramic view of hamburger

stands, or cafe-gas stations, in general, along Highway 66. They all look alike. Minnie or Susy or Mae are "middle-aging behind the counter" while Joe or Carl or Al, wearing the white cook's hat, slap down hamburgers. In the same paragraph Steinbeck moves smoothly from the general to the specific. "He [Al] repeats Mae's orders gently, scrapes the griddle, wipes it down with burlap. Moody and silent" (p. 209).

From now on to the end, the chapter is a narrative of its own, involving Mae and Al and the people who stop at their stand. There are frequent intercalary paragraphs that serve to unify the chapter and also to relate it to the whole book.

Mae, who is the contact with the public, shows a definite preference for truck drivers, who constitute the backbone of the regular trade. When they come she exchanges banter and rough jokes with them. Al never speaks; he is content; he cooks. In the meantime traffic is constant: "Cars whisking by on 66. License plates. Mass., Tenn., R.I., N.Y., Vt., Ohio. Going west. Fine cars, cruising at sixty-five" (p. 210).

Nine brief intercalary paragraphs follow depicting an imaginary conversation between any group of customers at any of the hamburger stands, remarking on the different kinds of cars from Cords to jalopies, their speed and merits.

A fuller intercalary paragraph describes the "Languid, heat-raddled ladies" (p. 210) who ride in big cars, laden down with accoutrements to improve their looks, move their bowels, insure their sex life being unproductive—all apart from their clothes. Artificiality and sterility have long since stifled any regenerative life force here. The description continues in two additional intercalary paragraphs: one, still on women in big cars who are bra-ed, girdled, sullen, discontented, selfish, and bored; the other, on men who accompany such women, men who are pot-bellied, puzzled, worried, insecure, but who are reassured in lodges and clubs that business is "not the curious ritualized thievery they know it is" (p. 211).

Then Steinbeck focuses on one woman and one man, going to California, just for the sake of being able to return home and say they had been there, casually dropping Hollywood gossip for effect. They cruise along at sixty in a big car. The woman, wanting a drink, wonders if it would be clean in this godforsaken country. She is typical of the Ugly American who travels and complains of facilities. When they stop at Al and Mae's, a personalized couple of the stereotyped rich come together with a personalized couple of the hamburger stand owners. The customers order very little, but complain and make themselves generally obnoxious, and then go on. Mae had seen this type of customer, when she worked in a hotel in Albuquerque, carry off towels, soap dishes, anything. She prefers truck drivers and hopes that the approaching transport will stop.

Then follows a conversation between a truck driver, Big Bill, and his helper, who plan to stop at Al and Mae's, and do. Big Bill exchanges risque banter with Mae, telling off-color jokes while the helper puts a nickel in the phonograph, plays the slot machine and walks to the counter.

To Steinbeck, not all mechanization is bad. He mentions the sound of machines working to good advantage: the phonograph, the coffee urn, the ice machine, and the electric fan. In fact, earlier in Chapter 14, Steinbeck had an imaginary character ask, "is a tractor bad? Is the power that turns the long furrow wrong? If this tractor were ours it would be good" (p. 205).

Mae mentions that a Massachusetts car had stopped earlier. Big Bill says there are many cars, all going west. The helper describes a wreck they had seen that morning in which a fellow in a Cadillac, doing ninety, ploughed into a cut-down car full of family and household goods, killing one child, and filling the air with bedclothes, kids and chickens. In their general conversation they wonder where they all come from, where they all go; Mae repeats the rumor that the poor people steal, but she says that she and Al have lost nothing so far. Here is foreshadowing of the fear the local people come to have of the migrants as shown in the later chapters.

Just then a 1926 Nash pulls off to stop. The back seat is piled nearly to the ceiling with household stuff. Two boys are sitting on the load. With a mattress and a folded tent on top of the car, tent poles along the running board, a whole family and their possessions are in transit—like the Joads. A man gets out of the car, comes to the door and politely and humbly asks if he can get some water. The boys have already scrambled out and gone to the hose, and are digging their toes in the mud puddle. In Chapter 4 (p. 23), Tom Joad took his shoes off and worked his damp feet into the hot dry dust. In Chapter 30 (p. 616), Ma and Rose of Sharon "plowed through the mud." In many instances, throughout the book, the poor people stay in close touch with the soil.

After getting the water, the man wants to buy a loaf of bread for ten cents. Mae demurs—they would run short themselves and besides a loaf of bread costs fifteen cents. Threatened by growls, then snarls from Al if she doesn't, Mae sells them a loaf for ten cents, as well as two five cent sticks of candy for a penny. The man has his pride. He does not want charity, but he has far to go. (The Joads had to hoard their money. They had to turn Granma's body over to the authorities for a county burial, although Pa did pay five dollars to have a painted board put up [p. 341].) The Nash leaves the hamburger stand in a blue cloud, obviously burning oil. It is symbolic of all the jalopies in poor condition being nursed to get to California. (In the Joad family, Al assumes an importance a teen-ager might not otherwise have, for he knows about cars.)

The truck drivers have overheard the conversation in Al and Mae's place and when they go on their way they leave a generous tip. Mae contrasts them with the Massachusetts couple. (Ma Joad once mentioned that you will get help from your own people [pp. 513–514]. It was a truck driver in Chapter 2 who gave Tom a ride.) Al, the cook, has been generous, but he is also shrewdly calculating. He knows that it is time for the slot machine three to pay off so he plays it until it does, then puts the money in the till. Mae wonders what they'll do in California. Al asks, "Who?" Traffic continues to whiz by. Another transport stops and Mae goes into her routine of welcome.

Chapter 15 is not only a microcosm of *The Grapes of Wrath* but also a microcosm of the United States. Al and Mae's stand could have been on any highway. The rich, traveling in highpowered cars, crashed into poor families. The dispossessed and land hungry ones sought new homes but they still had their pride. They wanted work, not charity. Both generosity and selfish conniving came from unexpected sources. The artificiality and sterility of those removed from direct contact with the common segment of society is contrasted sharply with the persistence of the life force in the poor who ask for bread. The young boys looked at the candy not with any real hope but with great longing. The machine age uprooted man but it also brought changes that were beneficial. The big transports symbolized the far-reaching extent of commerce and trade, and they continued to come.

In looking back now on the structure of the book one can see the consistently worked out plan of alternating social and economic observations with chapters of a narrative, each augmenting the effect of the other, with a crystallization of the whole, placed in the center, confirming Steinbeck's own word that the structure was very carefully worked out.

LESLIE GOSSAGE ON DISCREPANCIES BETWEEN NOVEL AND FILM

Admittedly, much is lost from Steinbeck's work in Nunnally Johnson's script for Ford's film. The self-imposed Production Code of Hollywood joined with the faintly liberal politics of the filmmakers to erase the elaborate connections that Steinbeck develops between the private and the public—the lure of domination: the challenges of a woman hunted down or of an immense tract of land bought and paid for. Because of the Production Code and probably also because of their own sexual politics, the filmmakers could not include the farmyard jokes and anecdotes that in the novel so often express the inherent violence of patriarchal ownership—the desire to control land, animals, and women. They could not show the domestic violence at work in the changing relationship of Ma and Pa. They could not include Al's tomcatting and Tom's rebuke of him for it. They could not let us see the details of Rose of

Sharon and Connie's intimate relationship, nor her starved pregnancy, nor the enigmatic act of communal piety that ends Steinbeck's plot. Giving her breast to a starving tenant farmer creates an analogy between the personal and the political. Rose of Sharon and the farmer have both been abandoned by hierarchical powers—husband and corporate landowner. These powers have withheld the sustenance and security owed to wife and tenant for their subservience, their willingness to work, and the expected product of their labor. If either of them realizes that the patriarchal system itself is to blame and deserves destroying, the wine of rebellion will be served round. Steinbeck's novel suggests that the rapaciousness of human nature toward agricultural land and toward fellow beings is to blame for the socioeconomic crisis of farming in 1930s America, but the film touches on this constellation of ideas essentially not at all. In fact, the film's disclaimer prologue blames the weather.

Nonetheless, the film is a clear primer about the hard realities of day labor. Tom's understanding of the economics of his family's situation comes piecemeal from Muley and Casy and others; we absorb it as he does. Despite the prologue, the text of the film clearly aims an accusing finger at the banks and land companies unwilling to help the people who have worked the companies' lands for decades. We feel the indignant frustration of Muley and his son when they cannot find a human being to hold morally responsible for the disaster: "Well, who do we shoot?!" When the Joads find work we see them underpaid at the end of the day and overcharged at the company store. When the strike is broken, the scabs, the Joads among them, must take a fifty-percent cut in pay per box of peaches, just as Casy predicted. The Joads will now work all day for the same money that they had earned yesterday when they started work at midday. If yesterday's supper, bought with a half-day's earnings, left them hungry, there is no hope of eating adequately on the new lower pay. Their plan eventually to earn enough to buy a modest piece of land with a small white house seems more and more improbable. The film progresses relentlessly to the conclusion that Tom reaches under Casy's tutelage: Striking is the only way to struggle for their rights as human beings. The film realistically points out the greatest obstacle to a strike—the breadwinner's concern for the welfare of his own family. Granted that the film does not offer solutions to this conflict, it does show that the protagonist has become a zealot of workers' rights and intends to go off to try to find some solutions. In this way the film is politically radical, and belies the sentimental speech that Zanuck put in Ma's mouth as the last word of the film. Ma may think she should stay in her place, but the film's text has developed a radical rejection of this in Tom's character. *Grapes* stands near the beginning of a tradition of labor films including *On the Waterfront*, *Blue Collar*, *Norma Rae*, *Silkwood*, *Matewan*, and *Eight Men Out*.

(...)

By mixing expressionist narrative techniques with documentary cues and content, Ford keeps fiction and reality in constructive connection. The dark, expressionist sequences assert the inner life of the characters, balancing the distancing effects inherent in the external, opaque views of documentary style. The authors of the docubooks in the mid-1930s felt that the audience needed captions giving voices to the pictured people. The presentation of inner life through quotation—whether invented by Caldwell for Bourke-White's *You Have Seen Their Faces* or recorded at the moment of the photo taking and carefully transcribed by Taylor and Lange for *An American Exodus*—was considered an important addition to the possibly alienating surface of the person photographed. Through artistic conventions of narrative, Ford's film presents the inner lives of migrant characters so that the viewer, however prejudiced against the migrants' appearance, must admit having thoughts, concerns, and feelings in common with them.

Muley's memory sequence presents the blending of contrasting expressionist and documentary approaches. Tom Collins, the camp director of the actual Weedpatch camp and fellow traveler with Steinbeck among the migrants, received

$15,000 to be technical advisor to the filmmakers. The realism of the documentary details in the film are probably owing in great part to his contributions, as well as to Pare Lorentz's docufilms, *The Plow That Broke the Plains* and *The River*. Ford uses darkness in his expressionist sequences to evoke the contents of the mind—Tom walks around in his parents' house remembering. Muley begins telling his three-part story in the dark, but the story is brightly sunlit and in high contrast. Since high-contrast shooting was not common in Hollywood style in the 1930s, the viewer might easily associate that high-contrast look with the documentary photographs so common in books and photomagazines of the time. Muley knows about the economic facts of the evictions, so his speech also combines the emotional and the documentary. Muley is not an object acted on by document collectors, but a subject speaking, documenting his own story. The power of the sequence lies in the viewer seeing Muley from inside and outside at once. The only approach more powerful and true would be to have a migrant write and direct his own documentary narrative.

MIMI REISEL GLADSTEIN ON MA JOAD'S CHARACTER IN JOHN FORD'S FILM

Soon, *The Grapes of Wrath* may be watched as often as it is read. The power of visual images is strong. It is not unlikely that many people will substitute watching the film for reading the book. Therefore it seems appropriate, in view of this technological bonanza, to voice some misgivings about a troublesome aspect of the film that, though touched upon by a few critics, has not been thoroughly explored: John Ford's reduction and devitalization of the role of woman in his film version of *The Grapes of Wrath*. This enervation would be evident even if one were viewing the film without reference to the novel, but when the film is compared with the novel, the full dimensions of this diminishment are more clearly revealed.

Why Ford did this is not clear. It might have been a result of studio politics, of Ford's strong patriarchal bent, or of the practical constraints of film time. Whatever the reason, Ford reduced and softened the character of Ma Joad, and thereby diluted Steinbeck's depiction of woman's strength, durability, and significance in the human struggle for survival, a depiction that is distinctly embedded in the many layers, both realistic and mythic, of the book.[5] This diminishment of woman's character is also evident in Ford's version of Rose of Sharon, who in the book matures from a self-centered girl into a woman nearly ready to inherit Ma's mantle.

(...)

The Ma of director John Ford, screenwriter Nunnally Johnson, and actress Jane Darwell is a very different creature. Though she maintains a central role in the Joad saga, she is hardly the "citadel," in no way suggests a goddess, and her cohesiveness is a sticky sweet kind, like honey, instead of the fiercely binding kind practiced by Steinbeck's jack handle-wielding woman. She delivers the movie's message, but it, like the woman who speaks it, is a weaker, more conciliatory, Pollyannaish vision than the one posited by Steinbeck's Ma. Whatever plaudits the screen version of Ma has earned, as an interpretation of the novel's heroine she falls short on many counts.

The diminution of Ma begins with her first scene in the movie. In the novel, Tom hears Ma's voice before the reader is introduced to her by the narrator. Her voice is "cool ... friendly and humble." Her first words reflect her hospitality. Without knowing who the "coupla fellas" are who "wonder if we could spare a bite," she responds with an immediate "Let 'em come." This, although the Joads have just lost their homes and have little to sustain them on their impending journey. Ma's strong sense of sharing with strangers in this scene foreshadows her behavior in inviting Casy along with the family. Neither action is shown in the film. In the novel Casy asks Ma, Grandpa, and Tom if he can go along. When none of the men answers, it is Ma who tells Casy she would be proud to have him along. Later, in the family council, when Pa worries about the extra mouth to feed, it is Ma who firmly pronounces the code of hospitality and neighborliness: "I never heerd tell of no Joads or no Hazletts, neither, ever refusin' food an' shelter or a lift on the road to anybody that asked" (139). A sense of community that reaches beyond the boundaries of kinship is an important aspect of Steinbeck's message, a message that is considerably blunted in the movie. Cutting out Ma's articulation of these values early in the film presages their loss in the rest of the script.

(...)

The first glimpse of the movie Ma is of Jane Darwell standing by the family ta ble. The commanding presence in the room is not Ma, but Grandpa. Charley Grapewin's Grandpa, whether quarreling with Grandma or imagining himself sitting and "scrooging around" in a tub of grapes, steals this scene, even from such traditional scene-stealers as the children.[10] Darwell's Ma is a soft and dumpy-looking woman. Just in terms of outward appearance, she is a great disappointment. Russell Campbell tells us that John Ford would have preferred Beulah Bondi's "gaunt, stringy resilience" in the role, but had to accept Jane Darwell in return for getting Henry Fonda to play Tom instead of Don Ameche or Tyrone Power, whom the studio had on hand as contract players.[11] John Baxter concedes that Jane Darwell is "perhaps too plump, too matriarchal, too *Irish* for her role," but he counters that "so effective is Ford's use of the actress that one can no longer imagine anyone else playing it."[12] Baxter's point is a good one, but I think it has more to do with the impact of visual images than with the limits of imagination. It is just such concession to the power of the movie that I am arguing against.

(...)

In the novel there are many occasions where Steinbeck shows us Ma's assertive strength and sagacity. The aggressive nature of Ma's strength even becomes an occasion for jokes. Tom teases Al that he better have the truck ready or "I'll turn Ma on ya" (481). The stick scene is in neither screenplay nor film. Its loss is not crucial in and of itself, except when added to the loss of other scenes that illustrate Ma's assertiveness, natural wisdom, and family authority. The combined losses significantly affect the nature of Ma's character. Ford's Ma is sweet, good, and reassuring, but there is little evidence that she understands their situation, nor is she assertive about her beliefs. She does not act to effect her values.

Her lack of action helps account for much of the devitalization of the image of woman in the movie. The movie Ma does not determine the judgment of the family council about Casy's accompanying them, she does not face down the company store clerk, she does not wield a jack handle to keep the family together, and she does not threaten Pa with a stick to anger him lest he become too dispirited. All such scenes in which Ma acts assertively are absent from the movie.

Not only is the movie Ma less active than Steinbeck's Ma, but she also understands less. In the film, one of Ma's major speeches comes after Tom has killed the deputy who killed Casy. Tom wants to run away, but Ma wants him to stay and help her with the family. She begins the speech with the statement "They's a whole lot I don't understan'" and then bemoans the loss of land and traditions that bound the family together. Darwell's Ma is both nostalgic, her eyes cast on faraway sights, and pleading, she needs Tom to stay and help her.[16] Her pleas are effective. Tom does stay, and they go on to a better situation, the Weedpatch camp. The same speech in the novel has a different context. First of all, Ma is questioning Tom about Casy's death. She wants to know how and why it happened and what Casy said. The significance of Casy's Christ-like final words, "You don' know what you're a-doin'," is not lost on Ma. She repeats the words and exclaims, "I wisht Granma could a heard" (535).

(...)

Steinbeck's early novels, with their terse, dramatically developed plots, lend themselves well to the film medium. His scenes can often be lifted directly from the page to the screen.

And the best screenwriters did just that. It is possible that an actress such as Beulah Bondi could have translated both the physical and spiritual strength of Steinbeck's Ma Joad. With her in the role, the jack handle scene might have been retained. But production decisions prevented this possibility and we are left with a fine, but flawed, film. John Ford's *The Grapes of Wrath* has many excellences. Still, as the story of humanity, the story of family, it grossly underplays the role of half the human race. One is left disappointed by the devitalization and diminishment of Ma Joad, one of the American novel's most admirable and engaging heroines. The women in the film are soft, sweet, passive, and long-suffering—nurturers, but not leaders in the struggle for survival. Steinbeck's women, though few in number, are strong in significance. They are tough as well as tender, feisty, and assertive. Though often helpless against overwhelming odds, they do more than mouth platitudes. At the end of Steinbeck's *The Grapes of Wrath* it is Ma Joad and Rose of Sharon who serve as both the symbols and the actors in human survival.

Notes

5. Steinbeck says that there are five layers to the book and that the reader can participate to the level of his or her depth or hollowness. Letter to Pascal Covici, 16 January 1939, in *Steinbeck: A Life in Letters*, 178.

10. Andrew Sarris says it is no accident that this scene is dominated by Charley Grapewin's Grandpa while scenes between Jane Darwell's Ma and Russell Simpson's Pa are dominated by Darwell (*John Ford Movie Mystery*, 97).

11. Campbell, *Modern American Novel and the Movies*, 109.

12. John Baxter, "The Grapes of Wrath," in *The International Dictionary of Films and Filmmakers: Volume 1*, ed. Christopher Lyon, 185 (Chicago: St. James Press, 1985).

16. Warren French is so unsympathetic and out of patience with Jane Darwell's Ma that his description of this scene reads, "the camera jumps nervously about as Ma rattles [emphasis mine] on about her need for help" (*Filmguide to "The Grapes of Wrath"* [Bloomington: Indiana University Press, 1973], 51).

Works by John Steinbeck

Cup of Gold, 1929

The Pastures of Heaven, 1932

To a God Unknown, 1933

"The Murderer," 1934

Tortilla Flat, 1935

In Dubious Battle, 1936

"The Harvest Gypsies," (series on migrant workers published in the *San Francisco News*), 1936

Of Mice and Men, 1987

The Red Pony, 1937

The Long Valley, 1938

Their Blood is Strong, 1938

The Grapes of Wrath, 1939

Sea of Cortez (with Edward Rickets), 1941

The Moon Is Down, 1942

Bombs Away, 1942

Cannery Row, 1945

The Pearl, 1947

Burning Bright, 1950

East of Eden, 1952

Sweet Thursday, 1954

The Short Reign of Pippin IV, 1957

Once There Was a War, 1958

The Winter of Our Discontent, 1961

Travels With Charlie in Search of America, 1962

"Letters to Alicia" (for *Newsday*), 1965

America and Americans, 1966

Journal of a Novel: The "East of Eden" Letters, 1969

Annotated Bibliography

Astro, Richard, and Tetsumaro Hayashi, eds. *Steinbeck: The Man and His Work. Proc. Of the 1970 Steinbeck Conference.* Corvallis: Oregon State University Press, 1971.

This collection of articles, originally presented at the 1970 Steinbeck Conference held in Corvallis, Oregon, is written by an array of Steinbeck scholars and personal acquaintances.

Benson, Jackson J. *The True Adventures of John Steinbeck, Writer.* New York: Viking Press, 1984.

This PEN-award winning biography draws upon papers, photographs, and interviews to explore the many influences of Steinbeck's archetypal writing. It addresses his ongoing struggle for worker's rights, his often tenuous relationship with fame, his work in Hollywood, and the conflict he felt about the Vietnam War.

Brasch, James D. *"The Grapes of Wrath* and Old Testament Skepticism." *San Jose Studies*, 3, 2 (1977): 16–27.

This essay suggests that Steinbeck got his major ideas from Ecclesiastes: Casy was molded in the image of the preacher in the Old Testament, the migrants are similar to the Israelites, there are parallels between the Biblical promise that "the grapes of wrath" will one day ripen, and the solution to tyranny is in compassion and sympathy.

Con Davis, Robert, ed. *Twentieth Century Interpretations: The Grapes of Wrath.* Englewood Cliffs, NJ: Prentice-Hall, 1982.

This critical compendium begins with an introduction that traces the evolution of *The Grapes of Wrath* criticism from the initial, "hysterical reaction," as Peter Lisca calls it, to a more sound examination of structure, to a consideration of the novel as informed by epic and romance traditions. Includes essays by Lisca and George Bluestone.

Cook, Sylvia Jenkins. "Steinbeck, the People, and the Party," in Ralph F. Bogardus and Fred Hobson, eds., *Literature at the Barricades: The American Writer in the 1930s*. Tuscaloosa: University of Alabama Press, (1982): 82–95.

Cook compares *The Grapes of Wrath* to James Agee's *Let Us Now Praise Famous Men*—she looks through the lens of leftist literature in the 1930s and explores biological themes, including the phalanx, group man, and nonteleological thought.

Ditsky, John, ed. *Critical Essays on* The Grapes of Wrath. Boston: G.K. Hall and Co., 1989.

This work places the novel in historical perspective, with use of several illustrations and the reprinting of 10 reviews from 1939. Includes reviews by Louis Kronenberger and Philip Rahv and an essay by Jackson J. Benson.

Heavilin, Barbara A. John *Steinbeck's The Grapes of Wrath: A Reference Guide*. Westport, CT: Greenwood Press, 2002.

This examination of the novel first provides an overview of Steinbeck's family life and personal experience that draws heavily on his letters and journals. A detailed plot summary follows, as well as discussion of the sociocultural contexts behind his work and an examination of themes and motifs.

Levant, Howard. "The Fully Matured Art: *The Grapes of Wrath*," *The Novels of John Steinbeck: A Critical Study*. Columbia, MO: University of Missouri Press, 1974.

This essay suggests that *The Grapes of Wrath* symbolizes Steinbeck's attempt to write an epic in prose. Levant argues that Steinbeck is successful at elevating his story to universality in the first third of the novel, but in the last quarter he is reduced to allegory.

Lisca, Peter. *The Wide World of John Steinbeck*. New Brunswick, NJ: Rutgers University Press, 1958.

Addresses Steinbeck's novels in a chronological order so that readers may at once see the autobiographical connections to these works and the way that Steinbeck's writing evolves with the changing of his ideas, experience, and style.

Owens, Louis. *The Grapes of Wrath: Trouble in the Promised Land*. Boston: Twayne, 1989.

This book provides context for *The Grapes of Wrath*, including discussion and description of those families Steinbeck encountered during his research who later served as the inspiration for the Joad family. It also features an analysis of Steinbeck's early career and an overview of critical response to *The Grapes of Wrath*.

Parini, Jay. *John Steinbeck: A Biography*. New York: Henry Holt, 1995.

Parini explores Steinbeck's life and psychology by drawing on letters, interviews, and the controversy surrounding the quality of the man's writing, even as he earned such recognition as the Pulitzer and Nobel prizes. Emphasis on Steinbeck's slow and methodical discovery of his voice, as well as his relationships with people such as playwright Terrence McNally, actor Burgess Meredith, and especially his wives—Carol, Gwyn, and Elaine.

Steinbeck, Elaine and Robert Wallstein, eds. *Steinbeck: A Life in Letters*. New York: Viking Press, 1975.

This edited collection weaves together Steinbeck's autobiography by presenting—in chronological order—letters Steinbeck wrote to his friends, family, and colleagues.

Valjean, Nelson. *John Steinbeck, The Errant Knight: An Intimate Biography of his California Years*. San Francisco: Chronicle Books, 1975.

This offering from a friend of Steinbeck chronicles the writer's life from his earliest days in Salinas, California. Valjean explores the connections between Steinbeck's characters and his life—including the hills he explored, the *paisanos* he drank with, and his relationship with Ed Ricketts.

Watkins, Floyd C. "Flat Wine from *The Grapes of Wrath*," in Barbara W. Bitter and Frederick K. Sanders, ed. *The Humanist in His World: Essays in Honor of Fielding Dillard Russell.* Greenwood, S.C., Attic, 1976.

In this essay, Watkins argues, in effect, that Steinbeck has not gotten his facts straight. Almost 20 inaccuracies exist in The Grapes of Wrath, according to Watkins—for example, the Joads, when cotton-picking, wouldn't have been paid by the acre, as Steinbeck suggests, but by the day.

Wyatt, David, ed. *New Essays on* The Grapes of Wrath. New York: Cambridge University Press, 1990.

Wyatt characterizes the three phases of response to *The Grapes of Wrath* into the "Histrionic, the Formal, and the Contexual," or "Pretext (1940–1955), Text (1955–1973); and Context (1973–1989)." The essays in this volume cover issues of Steinbeck's politics, views of women, and the transformation of the novel into film.

Contributors

Harold Bloom is Sterling Professor of the Humanities at Yale University. He is the author of over 20 books, including *Shelley's Mythmaking* (1959), *The Visionary Company* (1961), *Blake's Apocalypse* (1963), *Yeats* (1970), *A Map of Misreading* (1975), *Kabbalah and Criticism* (1975), *Agon: Toward a Theory of Revisionism* (1982), *The American Religion* (1992), *The Western Canon* (1994), and *Omens of Millennium: The Gnosis of Angels, Dreams, and Resurrection* (1996). *The Anxiety of Influence* (1973) sets forth Professor Bloom's provocative theory of the literary relationships between the great writers and their predecessors. His most recent books include *Shakespeare: The Invention of the Human* (1998), a 1998 National Book Award finalist, *How to Read and Why* (2000), *Genius: A Mosaic of One Hundred Exemplary Creative Minds* (2002), *Hamlet: Poem Unlimited* (2003), and *Where Shall Wisdom be Found* (2004). In 1999, Professor Bloom received the prestigious American Academy of Arts and Letters Gold Medal for Criticism, and in 2002 he received the Catalonia International Prize.

Sarah Robbins has an MFA in fiction writing from New School University. She is a New York City-based writer and editor. Her nonfiction has appeared in *American Book Review*, *ArtNews*, *Glamour*, and *Newsday*.

Stanley Kunitz is the author of many books of poetry, including *Selected Poems, 1928–1958*, which won the Pulitzer Prize. In 2000 he was named U.S. Poet Laureate. He taught for many years in the writing program at Columbia University, and his honors include a Ford Foundation grant and a Guggenheim Foundation fellowship.

John Ditsky has written more than 100 critical articles and essays, with a concentration on the works of John Steinbeck.

The author of *Essays on East of Eden, John Steinbeck: Life, Work, and Criticism*, and *The Onstage Christ*, Ditsky has also published three volumes of poetry, the most recent of which is *Friend & Lover*. He teaches at the University of Windsor in Ontario, Canada, where he also serves as poetry editor for *The Windsor Review*.

Brian E. Railback was the founding dean of The Honors College and head of the English Department at Western Carolina University. He is the author of *Parallel Expeditions: Charles Darwin and the Art of John Steinbeck* and is co-editor of *A John Steinbeck Encyclopedia*.

Malcolm Cowley worked as assistant editor at the *New Republic* from 1929 to 1944 and edited the works of Ernest Hemingway, William Faulkner, and Nathaniel Hawthorne. He is the author of many works of literary criticism, essays, and poetry, as well as the autobiographical Exile's Return.

Frederic I. Carpenter was a professor at the University of Chicago and Harvard University. He is the author of *Emerson and Asia*, *Metaphor and Simile in the Minor Elizabethan Drama*, and *Eugene O'Neill*.

J. Paul Hunter is the former chair of the English department at Emory University. He is the author of *The Reluctant Pilgrim*, *a study of Robinson Crusoe* and the editor of *Forms of Prose Fiction*.

Nellie Y. McKay is co-editor with Henry Louis Gates, Jr. of the *Norton Anthology of African American Literature*; author of *Jean Toomer, The Artist: A Study of His Literary Life and Work*; editor of *Critical Essays on Toni Morrison*; and co-editor of the *Norton Critical Edition of Harriet Jacobs's Incidents in the Life of a Slave Girl; Approaches to Teaching the Novels of Toni Morrison*, and *Beloved: A Casebook*.

Warren French is the chair of the American Studies Department at Indiana University/Purdue University at Indianapolis. He is the author of an introduction to Steinbeck's *In Dubious Battle*, *John Steinbeck's Fiction Revisited*, and *John Steinbeck's Non-Fiction Revisited*.

Stuart L. Burns teaches 20th-century American literature at Drake University in Des Moines, Iowa. He is the author of *Whores Before Descartes: Assorted Prose and Poetry*

Edwin T. Bowden teaches American literature at the University of Texas, Austin. He has published numerous articles and books and is the textual editor of a new scholarly edition of the works of *Washington Irving*.

Mary Ellen Caldwell is an Emeritus Professor at the University of North Dakota, specializing in 19th-century literature.

This extract by **Leslie Gossage** is taken from the Gossage's longer essay "The Artful Propaganda of Ford's The Grapes of Wrath" as it appeared in *New Essays on* The Grapes of Wrath published by Cambridge University Press.

Mimi Reisel Gladstein is a Professor of English and Theatre Arts at the University of Texas at El Paso, where she is currently Associate Dean of Liberal Arts. She is the author of *The Ayn Rand Companion* (1984), *The Indestructible Woman in Faulkner, Hemingway, and Steinbeck* (1986), *The New Ayn Rand Companion, Revised and Expanded Edition* (1999), and a volume on *Atlas Shrugged* for Twayne's Masterwork Studies series, *Atlas Shrugged: Manifesto of the Mind* (2000). She has won the John J. and Angeline Pruis Award for Steinbeck Teacher of the Decade (1978–1987) and the Burkhardt Award for Outstanding Contributions to Steinbeck Studies in 1996.

Acknowledgments

"Wine out of These Grapes" by Stanley Kunitz. From *Wilson Library Bulletin*, 14 (October 1939), © 1939 by The H.W. Wilson Company. P. 165. Reprinted by permission of the Wilson Library Bulletin.

"The Ending of The Grapes of Wrath: A Further Commentary" by John Ditsky. From *Critical Essays on Steinbeck's* The Grapes of Wrath. © 1989 by G.K. Hall. Reprinted by permission of The Gale Group. Revised from *Angora*, 2 (Fall 1973), © 1973 by Agora. Pp. 41–50.

"The Darwinian Grapes of Wrath" by Brian E. Railsback. From *Parallel Expeditions: Charles Darwin and the Art of John Steinbeck*, © 1995 by the University of Idaho Press. By permission of University of Idaho Press, Moscow, Idaho.

"American Tragedy" by Malcolm Cowley. From the *New Republic*, 98 (3 May 1939), © 1939 by the New Republic. Pp. 382–383. Reprinted with permission of the New Republic.

"The Philosophical Joads" by Frederic I. Carpenter. From *College English*, 2(4), January 1941, © 1941 by the National Council of Teachers of English. Pp. 315–325. Reprinted with permission.

"Steinbeck's Wine of Affirmation" by J. Paul Hunter. Pp. 39-42, 46–47. *Twentieth Century Interpretations of* The Grapes of Wrath, edited by Robert Con Davis. (Englewood, NJ: Prentice Hall, Inc., 1982). Originally published in Langford, Richard E. (editor). *Essays in Modern American Literature*. DeLand, Florida: Stetson University Press, 1963.

"Happy[?]-Wife-and-Motherdom" by Nellie Y. Mckay. From *New Essays on* The Grapes of Wrath. Pp. 58–59, 65–67. Copyright © 1990 Cambridge University Press. Reprinted with permission of Cambridge University Press.

"John Steinbeck and Modernism (A Speculation on His Contribution to the Development of the Twentieth-Century American Sensibility)" by Warren French. From *Steinbeck's Prophetic Vision of America*, ed. Tetsumaro Hayashi and Kenneth D. Swan, © 1976 by Taylor University for John Steinbeck Society of America. Pp. 35–55. Reprinted with permission.

"The Turtle or the Gopher: Another Look at the Ending of The Grapes of Wrath" by Stuart L. Burns. From *Western American Literature* 9 (1974), © 1974 by Western American Literature. Pp. 53–57. Reprinted with permission of the editors.

"A New Consideration of the Intercalary Chapters in The Grapes of Wrath" by Mary Ellen Caldwell. From the *Markham Review* 8 (1973), © 1973 the Markham Review. Pp. 115–119. Reprinted with permission of the editor and author.

"The Commonplace and the Grotesque" by Edwin T. Bowden. From *The Dungeon of the Heart* by Edwin T. Bowden, © 1961 by Edwin T. Bowden. Pp. 138–149. Reprinted with the permission of Scribner, an imprint of Simon & Schuster Adult Publishing Group.

"The Artful Propaganda of Ford's The Grapes of Wrath" by Leslie Gossage. From *New Essays on* Grapes of Wrath. Pp. 101–104, 115. © Cambridge University Press 1990. Reprinted with permission of Cambridge University Press.

"From Heroine to Supporting Player: The Diminution of Ma Joad" by Mimi Reisel Gladstein. From *Critical Essays on Steinbeck's* The Grapes of Wrath. © 1989, G.K. Hall. Reprinted by permission of The Gale Group. Pp. 124–137.

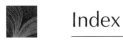

Index